CW00409438

MA

Waverley Abbey Resources is a trading name of CWR.

© CWR 2020.

CWR, Waverley Abbey House, Waverley Lane, Farnham, Surrey GU9 8EP, UK Tel: 01252 784700

Email: mail@waverleyabbey.org Registered Charity No. 294387. Registered Limited Company No. 1990308.

Unless otherwise indicated, all Scripture references are from the Holy Bible: New International Version (NIV), copyright © 1979, 1984 by Biblica. Used by permission of Hodder & Stoughton Publishers, an Hachette UK company. All rights reserved. Other versions used are marked: Holy Bible, New Living Translation, copyright © 1996, 2004, 2015 by Tyndale House Foundation. Used by permission of Tyndale House Publishers, Inc., Carol Stream, Illinois 60188. All rights reserved.

Where possible, every effort has been made to ensure that these devotional notes contain the correct permissions and references. Please contact the Publisher directly for any further permissions information.

Cover image: iStock

Printed in England by Linneys

MIX
Paper from responsible sources
FSC® C015900
www.fsc.org

WAVERLEY ABBEY
RESOURCES

Every Day with Jesus is available in large print from Waverley Abbey Resources. It is also available on **audio** and **DAISY** in the UK and Eire for the sole use of those with a visual impairment worse than N12, or who are registered blind. For details please contact **Torch Trust for the Blind**, Tel: 01858 438260. Torch House, Torch Way, Northampton Road, Market Harborough LE16 9HL.

MONDAY 1 MARCH

Night Visitor

Nicodemus came to Jesus at night and said, 'Rabbi, we know that you are a teacher who has come from God.' John 3:2

Waking in the dead of night is awful. Here we're confronted with our darkest thoughts. I note it was a sleepless Nicodemus who visited Jesus at night.

Darkness intensifies our loneliness, yet also protects us from the scrutiny we fear. Respectable Nicodemus emerges from the shadows to approach the less than respectable Jesus.

He asks his question. Jesus pauses to consider if this is flattery, or an honest enquiry? Lost in his internal darkness, Nicodemus hungers for more understanding.

Darkness engulfs us all from sunset to sunrise. It's a space all too often filled with the conflicts that map our lives. Uncertain of tomorrow's promise, we remain dissatisfied with yesterday's realities.

Must my yesterdays always shape my tomorrows? A question that haunts us all. Change challenges comforting certainties. Yet, until and unless I change, I cannot grow in my friendship with God. Nothing is as frightening as being besieged by uncertainty. My darkest fears stalk me, testing my resilience, my confidence and my God.

Then I hear the faintest call: *'Come, follow me'*. My life's disrupted. God's voice is familiar but my path obscure. I'm drawn in God's direction, but fearful of having to redirect my steps. My carefully crafted life plan now subject to change or rewriting. It's mission no longer my own but one commissioned by God; one I cannot fathom until I embark upon it.

Failure to respond leaves me a dissatisfied wanderer in a wilderness of my own confusion. Now I must summon my inner resolve and call out to God, my only source of light. Moving on proves challenging. I haven't the coordinates for my destination. God looks only for my obedient response. I waver between yes and perhaps.

SOMETHING TO CONSIDER: What disturbs you within your Christian faith?

AN ACTION TO TAKE: In the darkness first acknowledge your fear, then choose to follow Jesus, then seal this with a prayer.

A PRAYER TO MAKE: 'Lord, meet me in the dark and lead me towards the light each and every day.'

Wellness

Jesus replied, 'I tell you the truth, unless you are born again, you cannot see the Kingdom of God.' John 3:3

Wellness products cry out for my attention today. They all share one promise: changing my life for the better. Yet, why am I drawn to such promises? Well, we're continually looking outside ourselves for meaning, and in response there's been an explosion of courses offering self improvement to realise full potential.

This market plays upon humanity's disease of dissatisfaction. After childhood we begin to look for external cues as to how to present ourselves to ensure a fulfilled and fulfilling life. Nicodemus, perceived as a successful Jew, serving as a respected member of the ruling Jewish Council, still knew deep within that he remained dissatisfied. Seeing the miraculous works of Jesus. and worshipping a God of the miraculous, he dared to believe this might indeed be God in the flesh.

Finding the courage to approach Jesus, he's presented with a riddle, one that's common to us all. If we are to discover who we are truly born to become we must first find the courage to reawaken the hope that once fuelled our imagination. The bland, uncompromising pressures of contemporary life seek to squeeze every last drop of hope from our souls. Yet, once we catch sight of God, we dimly perceive a Kingdom that is not of this world. What will it take to exchange the dull monotony of a prefabricated life for one that we design for ourselves?

It begins with new birth that transforms the lens through which we view ourselves and our world. A view that is only available through the promise of God alone, promises presented in God's Word. An encounter with our Creator, who we first make peace with, and who then empowers us to become the person deep inside we always knew we were created to be.

SOMETHING TO CONSIDER: Who is the person you have suppressed whilst finding your place in this world?

AN ACTION TO TAKE: Discover God's Plan for Your Wellbeing.
Visit **edwj.org/ma21-2mar**

A PRAYER TO MAKE: 'Lord, I no longer want to be conformed to the constraints of this world. I choose to be transformed by Your promise of fullness of life.'

WEDNESDAY 3 MARCH

Mystery

'What do you mean?' exclaimed Nicodemus. 'How can an old man go back into his mother's womb and be born again?' John 3:4

Mystery lies at the heart of faith. It presents an obstacle to belief. How can I believe something I cannot comprehend? Nicodemus' reaction reveals the intense frustration that burns in his heart. He hears, yet does not understand.

Whilst there is a rational basis for Jesus' credentials as Saviour and Lord, placing my complete trust in him is irrational, i.e. beyond reason.

Jesus makes no apology. We must all wrestle with being born again. We may not literally return to our mother's womb, yet in every other aspect of our understanding we return to infancy.

My accumulated knowledge and skills still serve me, but bring me no closer to God. The world that has shaped my understanding to date is of no value in comprehending an unseen Kingdom awaiting full realisation.

Am I willing to explore entrusting who I am completely to Jesus' promise of fullness of life? I most certainly long for inner fulfilment. To enjoy being at peace with myself and my circumstances is a prize worth seeking.

So for Nicodemus the price is the disturbance of rethinking his entire worldview. The very foundation and currency of his life and relationships. The fabric of his social framework. Everything in a moment is shaken. The substance of his life threatens to collapse, leaving him naked and vulnerable; just like a newborn.

If we are to know, love and follow God, we must enter through the mystery of new birth. We must leave the safety of our comfort zone and deliberately enter into the learning zone. Here we are stretched, for everything we have used to construct our reality is subject to review. We choose to learn at a rate that best accommodates our own learning style. And slowly God's life of faith takes shape within and around us.

SOMETHING TO CONSIDER: How uncomfortable am I with my life? Am I still seeking God's fullness?

AN ACTION TO TAKE: Move from your comfort zone into the learning zone and address your discomfort.

A PRAYER TO MAKE: 'God, help me surrender all of my life to You, and learn to know and love You more.'

Crossing the Boundary

Jesus replied, 'I assure you, no one can enter the Kingdom of God without being born of water and the Spirit.' John 3:5

I srael faced an impenetrable boundary to escape captivity in Egypt, the Red Sea. I've discovered it's an experience we all must face if we're to make progress in our Christian life. I must confront my fear of the unknown. Crossing from the comfort to the learning zone awakens my fears and insecurities.

Yet, what's the alternative? Israel safely, and miraculously crossed the Red Sea to wander in a wilderness. Many soon craved the comfort of their former captivity. This despite its restraints and harsh conditions.

Faith can only ever be activated by the unknown. We experience discomfort, exchanging familiarity for risk. Yet, is familiarity our friend? It constricts our growth and limits our horizons. We become imprisoned by the good and prevented from experiencing the best.

Jesus invites us on a journey of discovery. Here we find the very best and worst of ourselves. We confront our addictions and the distractions seeking to direct our gaze away from God. We'll confront the limitations of our imagination that prevent us satisfying our deepest longings.

It took many years to recognise the many limits I placed on my Christian life. I was bound by inner fears: fears of making a mistake; failing God; becoming lost, or worse, trapped in a wilderness that might not sustain my life. Yet, this is to deny the promises of God. My challenge is the relentless pursuit of God towards the Promised Land. A journey that requires me to cross many boundaries, some apparently impenetrable.

I can't do it alone. My baptism declares my allegiance to Christ; it is my personal Red Sea experience. My guide must always remain the Spirit of God, that still small voice who, through prayer, convicts and convinces me of next steps in my quest to journey deeper towards the heart of God.

SOMETHING TO CONSIDER: What is my greatest fear that imprisons me in my comfort zone?

AN ACTION TO TAKE: Take a step into the unknown; a day course, a retreat, a Bible reading plan! Visit **edwj.org/ma21-4mar**

A PRAYER TO MAKE: 'Father, You know I trust You, yet I'm also uncertain if You will meet me in the wilderness I fear. Meet me at the boundaries of my life.'

FRIDAY 5 MARCH

Unpredictable

The wind blows wherever it wants. Just as you can hear the wind but can't tell where it comes from or where it is going, so you can't explain how people are born of the Spirit. John 3:8

Weather is unpredictable. Sun gives way to rain without warning. However we plan, we must always be prepared to be caught out. The Holy Spirit is much like the weather. We experience its effects but have no authority over its cause. The disciples, experienced sailors amongst them, were both caught out and terrified by a sudden storm on the familiar waters of Galilee. A storm that drove them to cry out to God, a cry God heeded. Once again we are presented with a fresh image of our inability to comprehend the full expression of God. Like Nicodemus, we feel our need and sense God's presence, yet prove incapable of comprehending it's meaning. Any attempt to reduce God's reality to a formula is doomed from the start. This does not make God capricious. Rather it reveals God's creativity. We remain no more than witnesses to the work of God in our own lives and in the lives of others.

It is this unique movement of God that invites response, and here Nicodemus wrestles with what he's to do. There are consequences. To resist the moment of God's invitation is to risk never encountering the wind of God's Spirit again. Yet, to respond and say yes is to voluntarily embrace change. I can of course hunker down and wait for the weather to pass, yet, like a tropical storm I experienced in Singapore, I may never encounter the experience again. I stood in a torrent of warm rain and was soaked to the skin. Then the rain stopped and within minutes I'd steam dried. I enjoyed it so much that I deliberately stood in the storm every afternoon until I returned to England. The moment of God's provocation can never be predicted. Will I respond or resist? I cannot know the consequences. Yet, will I ever encounter the opportunity again? Like Nicodemus we have a brief moment to make our decision.

SOMETHING TO CONSIDER: Are there moments of regret whenever I've declined God's invitation?

AN ACTION TO TAKE: Listen to those Holy Spirit hunches and respond positively; this is learning to live every day with Jesus.

A PRAYER TO MAKE: 'Father, sensitise me to the weather of Your Spirit so I might make appropriate decisions and make the most of my opportunities.'

Life in a Limitless World

'How are these things possible?' Nicodemus asked.
John 3:9

One thing's certain: life's full of questions. It's the basis for all learning. Knowledge is the fruit of our questions. So my questions reveal I'm an active disciple, or learner – the meaning of the word. Through meeting Jesus, Nicodemus decides to *follow* Jesus. Initial exasperation gives birth to fascination. One question leads to another. Satisfactory answers are in short supply but he's beginning a Christian walk.

Answers enable me to take control of my life. Yet, since I can never possibly find answers for all life's questions, I'm in danger of limiting my view within a limitless world.

Created in God's image, there are no limits on who I might become. In a material world we are deceived into thinking material success and security are the symbols of success. But not in Jesus' eyes.

One who chose to become poor that we might become rich, Jesus recognised that life is lost once we settle simply to serve individual need and desire. After all, Nicodemus had everything a man might desire: wealth, social status and all life's material benefits. Yet, within burned deep dissatisfaction that kept him awake at night knowing his many accomplishments left him with something he was still looking for.

His was a stark choice. Like the gambler with his last wager in hand, would he risk it on the final spin of the wheel? Whilst it felt like standing on the edge of ruin, in fact he stood at a point of finding what had always eluded him. Making peace with himself and finding a purpose that transcended life itself.

His question is posed and the wheel is spun. He stands at the point of no return; will he embrace Jesus or return to a secure, if unfulfilling, life? This question regularly faces each one of us.

SOMETHING TO CONSIDER: What's your biggest question, one you dare not ask?

AN ACTION TO TAKE: Find some creative way to step out of your comfort zone this week.

A PRAYER TO MAKE: 'Lord, I feel as if I have to let go of all I know if I am to take hold of all Your promise. Help me find courage to say yes to Your invitation for life.'

SUNDAY 7 MARCH

New Start

For this is how God loved the world: He gave his one and only Son. John 3:9

L ike Nicodemus, everyone is searching to satisfy an inner angst. So much is demanded of us from life that it's easy to lose touch with the 'real me' within. The popular TV programme *Escape Down Under* tells of families seeking a better life. They assume sun and sea offer them this opportunity. Yet, half return within a few years.

I once lived in Milton Keynes. Then a new city, it attracted many seeking 'a new start'. Once, I took a desperate phone call in the middle of the night from someone considering suicide. Their darkest fears were stalking them. Like Nicodemus, deeply disturbed, they urgently needed help.

Our lives are fragile, and short lived. Scripture describes them as like the grass and flowers that blossom for a brief summer before dying in the autumn. Beware of pushing anxiety into the future and refusing to face it head on. Like Nicodemus we may not find complete answers but we can fall in step alongside Jesus, who knows us and offers us hope in place of despair.

One reason I'm at Waverley Abbey is because it offers hope through Scripture, prayer, counselling and learning. It is a resource centre for all those with unresolved questions. It offers practical encouragement and support on-site and online.

When born again, we require support on our journey, for not one of us is an island. Waverley Abbey offers a vibrant community – both actual and virtual. We are here to welcome every Nicodemus in search of answers. Knowing where to turn is the first step in finding our way forward.

SOMETHING TO CONSIDER: Who do you have to encourage you in your walk of faith?

AN ACTION TO TAKE: Identify one practical resource that will support you in your Christian life.

A PRAYER TO MAKE: 'Lord, I know I cannot make it on my own. Help me build strong connections within the Christian community.'

Please write to me, **micha@edwj.org** with your questions and comments, and I'll write back personally and in confidence.

Become part of someone's testimony

Our Bible reading notes are read by hundreds of thousands of people around the world, and *Every Day with Jesus* and *Inspiring Women Every Day* have recently been made free in the UK. We want everyone, whatever their financial means, to have access to these resources that help them walk each day with our Saviour.

Here's what one *Every Day with Jesus* reader wrote to us:

Ever since I started using Everyday with Jesus, I reconnected to the Lord directly again. It deals with my day to day and minute to minute problems in details. Guiding me in the most solemn and right direction for a dedicated Christian living.

As we trust in God's provision, we know there are costs to providing this ministry. Do you have a passion for God's Word changing lives? Could supporting this vision be a way in which you serve?

A gift of just £2 a month from you will put daily Bible reading notes into the hands of at least one person who is hungry to know God and experience His presence every day.

Visit **waverleyabbeyresources.org/donate** to become part of someone's testimony, or use the form at the back of these notes.

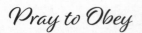
Pray to Obey

> **Satan said to the woman, 'Did God really say, 'You must not eat from any tree in the garden'?'** Genesis 3:1b

Rivers of ink have been spilt writing about prayer. Yet, we remain uncertain in our prayers. Do I pray enough? Why doesn't God answer me? Isn't it better to *do* something than to pray something? It's difficult to find useful answers to our ceaseless questions.

Here at the start of the Bible we discover our critical problem. We can only ever know God is all good if we've something evil to contrast goodness with. It emerges in the form of Satan. Eve faces a question and a choice. She feels obligated to answer, for herself if no one else. Yet, some questions have no answers; they merely define the landscape of our life. Prayer is essential in contesting the instability born of unanticipated questions. Some elements of learning require questions posed, then explored and answered; others merely seek to undermine my confidence in who I've chosen to believe.

Growing up, one of the biggest challenges was resisting peer pressure when it pushed me towards disobeying my parents. There were always compelling reasons to follow my peers, rather than my absent parents.

I experienced an intense inner conflict and, no matter which way I eventually moved, I was left dissatisfied; either disappointing parents or friends. And then of course there was the secrecy. I was no longer able to live in a transparent relationship with my family. I entered the murky world of deceit, both of myself and others.

Prayer offers that pause when we choose to turn to God and consider what is our best course of action. Prayer offers moments of consideration before we act. It is indispensable if we are to follow Jesus effectively. History so often hinges upon our prayers, either said or left unsaid. It's why prayer continues to provide the heart of Waverley Abbey's ministry.

SOMETHING TO CONSIDER: What specifically prevents me from praying?

AN ACTION TO TAKE: Agree with yourself to pray the Lord's Prayer on waking each morning.

A PRAYER TO MAKE: 'Lord, forgive me when I use reason to do what I choose without first pausing to pray'.

Lift Up Your Voice!

The man and the woman hid from the Lord God among the trees of the garden. Genesis 3:8b

Earlier this year Jayne, my wife, had Covid-19. No temperature and no cough, but a loss of voice. Directed to A & E, Coronavirus was confirmed and she was sent home. She was aware she was unwell before symptoms and diagnosis but couldn't precisely say what the problem was.

How like us. We feel out of sorts with God, ourselves and others, yet can't quite locate why. Here Adam and Eve, having followed their own reasoning, instinctively feel they must hide from God. The problem with disobeying God is that we carry an awareness of it deep within. We feel too ashamed to face God and seek forgiveness. We even attempt to justify our wrongs.

Whatever justifications we attempt to give to wrongdoing, we can never escape that gnawing inner sense of shame. Of course we seek to face it down and minimise its importance together with the scars it leaves within. Yet, eventually we must face the consequences. And there are always consequences.

Inner conviction is perhaps the most important guide directing us to prayer. If we feel discomforted then, rather than hide and hope, we must return to God, much as Jayne made her way to A&E.

One essential way we do this is to pray and in so doing lift our voice and open our heart to God. Express regret and disappointment whilst seeking to recover our friendship. Failure to do so only leaves us naked and alone in the undergrowth of our own self-deception.

Although observers need never know of the struggles and justifications we carry within, we remain naked before God and self until we make our peace with God. It is God alone who can clothe us in our right mind.

SOMETHING TO CONSIDER: What are you seeking to hide from God, and yourself?

AN ACTION TO TAKE: Whenever you feel inner discomfort turn to God in prayer.

A PRAYER TO MAKE: 'Search me, God, and know my heart; see if there is any offensive way in me. Amen".'

*Psalm 139:23-24

WEDNESDAY 10 MARCH

Civil War

> **And I will put enmity between you and the woman, and between your seed and hers.** Genesis 3:15a

It was St. Paul who helpfully pointed out that we each struggle to do what we positively intend to do: *'For I do not do the good I want to do, but the evil I do not want to do – this I keep on doing'.*[1] There's a civil war waging within us!

This all relates back to the ground rules God established once Adam and Eve had reasoned their way out of God's provision. Having pursued Satan's logic, as opposed to God's wisdom, two clear options emerged as a consequence. Simply put: walking with God or away from God.

Here's where prayer helps. It expresses my commitment to pursue God. However, as a result of the enmity between God and Satan I often find it difficult to pray. How many times have I been distracted from actually praying when I meant to?

If we find the act of turning to prayer a challenge then we can be assured that we are following God. God's enemy deliberately seeks to sabotage our plans. In fact it's a life principle. Pursuing God will always mean I have to push back against 'good' reasons as to why NOW is not a good time to pray.

This enemy is like a virus and afflicts all of humanity. Therefore, prayer is in fact central to dealing with this human malady. It strengthens my resistance and prevents me becoming victim to the enemy's ceaseless demands. For if every moment is devoted to a distraction then my focus is never directed towards God. Satan has me imprisoned.

The history of the Church is one long account of the continuous prayer of God's people. A work that Waverley Abbey has embraced from its birth. If we are to celebrate the grace of God in every sphere of life, then we must invest our time and energy into prayer. This is the work of resistance that brings God's Kingdom on earth.

SOMETHING TO CONSIDER: What sabotages your commitment to prayer?

AN ACTION TO TAKE: Set a time each day, say ten minutes, when you will pray. Here are online resources to help: **edwj.org/ma21-10mar**

A PRAYER TO MAKE: 'Lord, help me as I choose to resist the devil, yield to you and pray.'

[1] Romans 7:19

Struggles

Cursed is the ground because of you; through painful toil you will eat food from it all the days of your life. Genesis 3:17b

Life is a struggle. Finding work to provide both a home and food consumes the largest percentage of our time. Without an income, life quickly collapses toward chaos. We fear financial instability for it threatens the very fabric of our identity.

Yet, work defined as physical and mental effort is a consequence of the conflict that exists in our world. Work is not bad, yet there are forms of employment that offer little personal fulfillment and may damage mental health. The way of the world means that we need to take any job, for without paid work life becomes impossible.

But complaint does not need to rule us, for we are invited to seek God in all that we do. God is not merely associated with the pleasures of life. This is good news in reality. It means wherever we find ourselves God is present and available. We just have to locate God.

It came as something of a shock when it first dawned upon me that life wasn't plain sailing. For a few years after conversion I carried a fiction in my head that now I loved God my difficulties were somehow behind me. In fact, one consequence of saying yes to God was that I found myself in more challenging circumstances.

In my frustration and confusion, in unanticipated and unwelcome circumstances, once I'd vented my fury and fears, I discovered that prayer was what I needed. It never gave a direct solution, yet calmed and focused me sufficiently to keep on after God without knowing when or how my life might change.

Prayer acts as a rudder keeping me upright in the storms of life. It also sends out the appropriate distress signal as I await much needed help if I'm to endure to the end.

SOMETHING TO CONSIDER: How do you choose to navigate the storms of life?

AN ACTION TO TAKE: Identify some key Christian friends who you can turn and talk to when enduring life's storms.

A PRAYER TO MAKE: 'Lord, help me to fix my eyes on Jesus as the one who will lead me from storm to safety.'

FRIDAY 12 MARCH

Birth pangs

Then the man named his wife Eve, because she would be the mother of all who live. Genesis 3:20

Within life there is a source of perpetual hope. While life is contested in so many ways, life is itself irrepressible. The circle of birth, life and death endlessly repeats providing chapter upon chapter of the invincible nature of the human spirit.

Prayer opens the window through which life floods in. Many have testified over the years to the presence of God born of prayer when in the most desperate of circumstances. It wasn't the circumstances that changed, but the individual's perspective of their circumstances.

Corrie Ten Boom, a great saint of God who endured Ravensbrück concentration camp, reminds us, 'You can never learn that Christ is all you need, until Christ is all you have'. Of course, who wants to reach the end of themselves to discover this truth? Good news! We never go in search of such experiences, yet if called upon to face them we are called upon to look for life amidst the pain.

Birth pangs accompany the delivery of every new life into this world. The phrase has now become associated with the disorder and distress associated with major social change. No wonder then that our desire for the life of God might lead us through some painful challenges.

In my own experience I vent at God, and others around me, because I, like you, do not enjoy pain. But this is pain that can bring me closer to God and enable me to realise the fullness of God in my life. In fact it is only the outworking of the promise I made to God when surrendering my life into His care at conversion. Pain forms an element along the way of discipleship. Indeed it's worth reflecting that God was incarnate through human birth: Jesus who would reverse the curse of the Fall and restore all who choose to follow in His footsteps.

SOMETHING TO CONSIDER: Where is God's life in the pain of your experience, both past and present?

AN ACTION TO TAKE: Journal your experience of pain in following Jesus at every step. It will become a testimony of God's grace.

A PRAYER TO MAKE: 'Lord, help me to hold everything in my hands lightly. I invite you to prise my fingers open whenever necessary.'

Unwavering

An extract from the introduction of Jen Baker's latest book

Unwavering
The power of choice

Jen Baker

One of the most profound truths in the Bible is that regardless of how we came into this world – whether by love, passion or violence – we were chosen. God is intentional and at the moment of creation you were not only His first choice, but His best choice. At birth, He knew the number of hairs on your head (or lack thereof) and the number of days before you. God is responsible for bringing us into the world, but what we do with that time – and the legacy we choose to leave – is solely our responsibility.

Choice was created at the birth of Creation. The first Hebrew word of the Bible means 'in the beginning' and the second means God *(Elohim)*, with the third word, *bara*, meaning 'created'. Any type of creation, whether we are creating a meal or a memory, involves choice. Therefore, Elohim chose, before

time was established, to express His love by appointing mankind as the recipient of His love; because love without an object to love is unfulfilled, empty and void of purpose. In other words, *you* are God's desire!...

My prayer is that as you read, fear will lose its grip, faith will come alive, and purpose will be realigned... positioning you for a lifetime of relentless, kingdom pursuit.

This is your time, and this is your choice – make it an unwavering one.

Want to keep reading?
Visit **waverleyabbeyresources.org.uk/products/unwavering** to continue.

SATURDAY 13 MARCH

Making Decisions

Also for the man and his wife the Lord God made tunics of skin, and clothed them. Genesis 3:21

Our popular image of right and wrong leads us to imagine right being rewarded and wrong punished. Yet, God doesn't operate on this polarity. Certainly there are consequences from bad decisions, yet these are less a punishment than a simple reality. King David's poor decision making had dire consequences, yet God still loved and blessed him with the title, a man after God's own heart.

There's always a temptation to wallow in self-pity once our indiscretion has been unearthed. As a child I remember sitting alone in my bedroom, where my parents' had sent me, fuming with self-righteous rage. Why is it I feel the need to justify my wrongdoing? All part of the tension between working with or against God.

Of course, the wonderful news is that God forgives and accepts those who regret their indiscretions and freely confess them. This was King David's path. Whilst he could not avoid the consequences, he was once again clothed in righteousness by God. Here Adam and Eve face the harsh truth following their poor choice. Yet even on the threshold of Paradise, God clothes them for the realities that lay beyond its gates.

Prayer serves us in recovering our relationship with God. Once the bravado of my self-righteousness wanes, I can drop to my knees and seek God's forgiveness. I do not need to twist God's arm; only admit my wrongdoing with integrity, ask forgiveness and redirect my steps as I continue God's way. We can never outrun God's grace; we can only choose to reject it and continue on our own. After confessing to God we exchange our rags for the fine clothing of humility, love and patience. God remains the finest fashion outfitter we can turn to.

SOMETHING TO CONSIDER: What 'clothing' do you want to pass on from your life?

AN ACTION TO TAKE: Jot down your own simple prayer of confession on your mobile and return to it regularly throughout your day. Read more about David, a sinner with God's heart. Visit **edwj.org/ma21-13mar**

A PRAYER TO MAKE: 'Lord, might I be swift in returning to You when I am wrong and recover grace.'

Work

The Lord God sent him out of the garden of Eden to till the ground from which he was taken. Genesis 3:23

Living with the consequences of poor decisions can prove challenging. Yet it requires the same mindset that we need for every one of life's eventualities: looking at my situation from God's perspective rather than my own.

Adam, now outside Eden, begins the challenge of grafting for his welfare. Work is never a bad thing, for indeed maintaining the garden of Eden required work. Yet now humanity must deal with the inner knowledge that evaluates the nature of the work undertaken. Is it fair? Is it appropriately rewarded? Are my rights sufficiently protected?

Satan continues to whisper in our ear, 'Has God said?' In other words we are tempted to look in various directions to secure what we believe to be our 'just desserts', yet more often than not we fail to look to God.

Adam is working the very ground from which his mortal frame had been taken. Indeed our mortality is never anything more than dust. It is only enlivened by God's Spirit. This same Spirit affords us the opportunity to look through the eyes of God at our every experience.

Our attention is much in demand, so we must choose to invest some of it learning God's way in God's world. Adam was at the starting gate and over time God's salvation plan would unfold. God also has a redemptive purpose for your life and mine. Our challenge is finding and focusing on it. At Waverley Abbey we offer practical resources to empower and encourage your personal pursuit of God. Jesus is God's Word and the Bible is the Word of God. I deliberately choose to meet Jesus daily in the Bible. I'd encourage you to begin there with *Cover to Cover*, a way to read the Bible in a year. And if you want to chat – email me: **micha@edwj.org**.

SOMETHING TO CONSIDER: How much work will you invest in building your friendship with God?

AN ACTION TO TAKE: Visit **waverleyabbeyresources.org** and choose one resource that will deepen your friendship with God.

A PRAYER TO MAKE: 'Lord, open my eyes daily that I may discover wonderful things in the Bible.'

MONDAY 15 MARCH

Majestic!

O Lord, our Lord, your majestic name fills the earth! Psalm 8:1a

The name of God is majestic; both beautiful and powerful. It commands our admiration, and while this is easily said, it's not always evident in our lived experience. God's majesty must be found. No wonder the Magi chose an arduous journey in search of the promised Messiah, the majesty of God. It's only by panning through much river dirt that one can find a gold nugget.

I often feel as though I'm living something of a 'rubbish' life. It's a powerful lie. I make critical assumptions born of observations and comparisons. Yet I can never know what anyone else is experiencing. Often my assumption is no more than a projection of my own dissatisfaction with my lot in life. During such unhealthy introspection I distract myself by enjoying the beauty of creation, itself a testimony to God's majesty.

Moving to St Cuthbert's Oratory some years ago we inherited a garden. Neither Jayne, my wife, nor I were gardeners. We both confessed to panicking on the eve of our move, fearing we would never manage the gardening.

Over the years we've worked hard creating a contemplative Godspace, which many come to and enjoy on quiet days and retreats. For each of us it's a place of grounding. When life begins to overwhelm me I walk the garden and deliberately commit to calming myself. Simply by observing the plants and trees I contemplate the wonder that is God at work in life. Plants can take no responsibility for their own growth or survival yet God ensures that what is barren today will flourish in due season.

The majesty of God Is revealed in the order of the seasons. Barrenness precedes fruitfulness. How often have we been tempted to remove a plant that looks all but expired only to marvel at its revival under God's timely care.

SOMETHING TO CONSIDER: Where do you find the majesty of God in your life?

AN ACTION TO TAKE: Visit or recall a natural landscape and consider the permanence and grandeur of our eternal God.

A PRAYER TO MAKE: 'Lord, I will look at your creation and it will instruct me. For the life of every living thing is in Your hand, and the breath of every human being.'*

*Job 12:20

Waverley Abbey College

Education that changes lives

Our programmes equip students with the skills and knowledge to release their God-given potential to operate in roles that help people.

Central to all of our teaching is the Waverley Integrative Framework. Built on 50 years of experience, the model emphasises the importance of genuineness, unconditional acceptance and empathy in relationships. The courses we offer range from certificates to Higher Education level.

Counselling

As society begins to realise the extent of its brokenness, we continue to recognise the need to train people to support those who are struggling with everyday life, providing training to equip individuals to become professional counsellors. Whatever their starting point in academic learning, we have a pathway to help all students on their academic journey.

Spiritual Formation

For those wanting to be better equipped to help others on their spiritual journey, this programme provides robust and effective Spiritual Formation training. Students engage with theology, psychology, social sciences, historical studies, counselling, leadership studies and psychotherapy.

For more information about all of our course offerings available, visit **waverleyabbeycollege.ac.uk**

TUESDAY 16 MARCH

Embrace God's Promise

Your glory is higher than the heavens. Psalm 8:1b

I note the word 'glory' is of uncertain origin. This is fitting for something that lies beyond our reach and comprehension as the heavens themselves. Glory indicates honour, splendour and fame. All of which are due to God. Yet, we discover God is never one to pursue self promotion. God's promises are revealed through the pages of Scripture, and ultimately in Jesus. The prophet Isaiah describes Jesus: 'There was nothing beautiful or majestic about his appearance, nothing to attract us to him. He was despised and rejected – a man of sorrows, acquainted with deepest grief. We turned our backs on him and looked the other way'.*

So glory appears to be turned on its head, reminding us that glory is encountered and experienced even in the most challenging circumstances. It's humbling to read the testimony of the persecuted. Many fail to see God's promise realised. Yet, like Isaiah, they see enough to maintain faith with little or no evidence to support their hypothesis.

It is this hypothesis, 'God with us, the hope of glory', that alone sustains our walk of faith. We must look beyond the natural realm and the wisdom of logic and reason if we are to embrace God's promise. At times I'm spiritually nauseous seeking to keep my eyes fixed on Jesus whilst all around me the storms of life threaten to overwhelm me.

Yet, I am not alone. I have as my companions those who have preceded me, the company of saints, as well as the loving, praying community of which I'm a member. Waverley Abbey is one such company. We exist to encourage a renewal of practical faith and practice throughout the world. Join us both for your own encouragement and to offer the encouragement of your prayer to others on this rocky road in the footsteps of Jesus.

SOMETHING TO CONSIDER: Can you discern Jesus walking towards you within the storm of your life?

AN ACTION TO TAKE: Join us in our commitment to world renewal through prayer, biblical literacy and learning, **edwj.org/ma21-16mar**

A PRAYER TO MAKE: 'Lord, when the road is rough and steep may I fix my eyes upon Jesus who alone has has power to keep me secure, a faithful friend upon whom I can depend.'

*Footnote: Isaiah 53:2–3, NLT

Change is Essential

You have taught children and infants to tell of your strength, silencing your enemies and all who oppose you. Psalm 8:2

It was the cries of the infant Moses floating in a reed basket that won Pharaoh's daughter's heart. She didn't realise this helpless baby would indeed silence the might of Egypt.

Similarly, Jesus was dismissed with Nathaniel's declaration, 'Can anything good come from Nazareth?'* Then he became Jesus' disciple. Never judge a book by its cover.

We too often disqualify ourselves from God's love as we assume our history and habits invalidate our discipleship. But God's never disillusioned with us for God never had any illusions in the first place. I can't prove my value to God. There is no pass mark to enter the Kingdom.

Children are far less self conscious than the adults they become. They believe they can move mountains. For this reason Jesus told us all to change and become children to enter God's Kingdom. Change is essential; a change of the lens through which I observe myself and my life.

Infants and children have little difficulty relying on those who care for them. A baby will wake you for food anytime of the day and night with no sense of embarrassment. It has no concept of the inner voices yet to emerge in adolescence. How often have I held back, altered course, allowed an opportunity to elude me due to those incessant inner voices?

Such voices are our greatest enemy. They restrict our capacity to pursue God. They domesticate our faith and we run the risk of reducing all Christian experience to mastering some assumed rules that we pray may define a quality of faith.

A cry like that of Moses will capture peoples' attention; it may position us to silence God's critics, those within and without.

SOMETHING TO CONSIDER: What are the voices that have encircled your life and domesticated your faith?

AN ACTION TO TAKE: Silence these inner voices by crying out to God and finding new confidence in God's living word, the Bible.

A PRAYER TO MAKE: 'Lord, help me to silence my inner critics. Enable me to find my voice, my true vocation.'

*John 1:46, NLT

THURSDAY 18 MARCH

God's Image

What are mere mortals that you should think about them?
Psalm 8:4a

God's concerned for the entire human race. Yet, remarkably, each of us can know and enjoy personal friendship with God. Only God has this capacity to include everyone and be intimately involved with each of us.

Whilst God is all sufficient without need of our companionship, God chooses to engage with us. This came at the cost of redemption through Jesus' life, death and resurrection. The psalmist's question is worth asking ourselves. God appears to have a higher regard for human welfare than we do, both for ourselves and our neighbours.

Every human bears God's image regardless of economics, ethnicity or gender. God sets the bar very high. So how can we love others less than this? In a world of suffering I'm invited to take seriously God's love for all humanity. I may not be able to change everyone's world everywhere, yet I can have a positive impact in someone's life somewhere.

This starts with the way I view and treat myself. I cannot love anyone else unless I respect and love myself. Failure here will mean I project my poor self image onto others and assume the worst of them. I won't find the best in them because I'm blinded to the best in me.

Being loved enables me to feel appreciated and valued. Medics note that babies starved of 'contact comfort', being held and touched, experience psychological damage.

So we must both marvel at God's love and establish our daily routine of 'comfort contact'. *Every Day with Jesus* offers just such a contact point. As does the app. *Lectio 365*, produced by 24-7 Prayer and Waverley Abbey. Ensure you maintain your 'comfort contact' as a child of God.

SOMETHING TO CONSIDER: Do I love and accept myself entirely, just as God loves and accepts me?

AN ACTION TO TAKE: Pass on a copy of *Every Day with Jesus* to a friend, colleague or family member. Download the app. *Lectio 365*,
edwj.org/ma21-18mar

A PRAYER TO MAKE: 'Lord, thank You for loving and accepting me. I choose to love myself and want to share that love with others.'

Friendship

What are human beings that you should care for them?
Psalm 8:4b

Maslow, in his hierarchy of needs, places care as priorities 1–3. They include our physiological and safety needs along with our need to be loved. Data detailing peoples' greatest fears highlight an inability to purchase food or provide a home, followed by a need for active relationships.

We're social by instinct. God created Eve for being alone isn't healthy. Lockdown has shown that loss of social interaction has a negative impact upon our mental health.

So friendship lies at the heart of God's appeal to us. Recognising mortal life is short, God invites us to enter into a friendship that's eternal. One that reaches beyond the grave.

All friendships take time to establish. They're subject to misunderstandings, periods of distance and dispute, an unwillingness to change and constant demands. Yet, such challenges forge a meaningful friendship.

Friendships are organic. They take shape and morph naturally over time. There is no formula on how to establish effective friendships. Any such attempts arise from a need to control the friendship for my advantage. That's not friendship, but a transaction.

It's why God gives us so much room. God has no desire or intention to control us. God recognises that we need the freedom to choose both to enter into friendship with God and the depth of friendship we desire.

As with all friendships, the deeper they go the more is demanded of each of us. This can prove daunting, yet we find a way to move on together because of that bond of friendship. It's why every day affords a new and exciting opportunity to discover more of both God and myself.

SOMETHING TO CONSIDER: How would I describe the depth of friendship I have with God?

AN ACTION TO TAKE: Decide, then make a note, how deep you want to go with God in your life.

A PRAYER TO MAKE: 'Lord, I need friendship and I accept your invitation to build a forever friendship with you, day by day.'

SATURDAY 20 MARCH

Global Imbalance

You gave them charge of everything you made, putting all things under their authority. Psalm 8:6

Many anguish over global imbalances. For some the inequality on our planet and in our society provides enough evidence to reject God. Yet, God has entrusted the world to our care.

In other words I live in a society that is the product of human effort. Where there's injustice it's a product of human decision making. We're asked to accept responsibility for the state of the world we live in.

However, I've grown up with a default inner reaction that seeks to lay blame for my problems at someone else's door. I'm often not even aware of my issues, only aware when they make their presence known usually by inconveniencing me.

My responsibility in such matters is twofold. Firstly I am to act in ways that encourage the quality of life I aspire to for myself and my family. It's no good speaking out against road rage if I'm as much a perpetrator as the victim. Action starts with my personal behaviour. And my behaviour as a disciple is clearly set out in Scripture. God even gifts me the fruit of the Spirit to help.

Such action can be followed up through participation in community activities and political engagement. Here I refuse to compromise my values whilst working for the benefit of others.

Secondly, I need to become consistent in prayer. Again many complain of unanswered prayer. Yet this might be looking through my own eyes alone. Prayer is in fact leaning upon God's grace to sustain God's purpose throughout God's world. Such a purpose is beyond my comprehension. Yet, voices raised in continuous prayer is one way God keeps the world turning and creates safe spaces. As disciples we are not called to a passive but to active faith and action.

SOMETHING TO CONSIDER: Are you practically active or inactive in your faith?

AN ACTION TO TAKE: Consider how you might participate and serve God's purpose around you.

A PRAYER TO MAKE: 'Lord, here I am. Send me.'

Please write to me, **micha@edwj.org** with your questions and comments, and I'll write back personally and in confidence.

WAVERLEY ABBEY

Find out more online

For more information and to make purchases of new books and courses or to take a look at the college courses and training that we offer, please take a look at our websites.

 waverleyabbey.org

 waverleyabbeyresources.org

 waverleyabbeycollege.ac.uk

 waverleyabbeyhouse.org

SUNDAY 21 MARCH

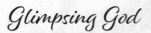
Glimpsing God

O Lord, our Lord, your majestic name fills the earth! Psalm 8:9

The final words of the psalm repeat its opening. The key difference is that we have discovered more of God and ourselves through its verses. We no longer simply look to the wonder of our natural world to catch a glimpse of God.

We now know that we ourselves are a real expression of that glory. Cracked vessels we most certainly are; yet it's through the cracks that God's light shines through most perfectly. We fill, or populate, the whole earth. We are God's glory within our workplace and neighbourhood. This is one way in which the earth is filled with the glory of God as the waters cover the sea. Remarkably each of us choosing to follow Jesus is an expression of God's good news on earth. We are living, breathing love letters spread throughout the earth; literally the hands and feet of Jesus and God's continuing mission of love in the world.

For this to happen it requires me to take three decisions. Will I choose to live my faith seriously? Will I become engaged in my worlds, both large and small, and actively participate in serving God's purpose? And finally, will I commit to pray daily for God's Kingdom to come on earth as it is in heaven?

Three big decisions that God invites you to consider. Decisions you must take alone, yet can only make happen in a practical way in companionship with others. Here at Waverley Abbey we exist to offer such companionship with resources, training and personal encouragement every step of the way. As Henry Ford said, 'Coming Together Is A Beginning; Keeping Together Is Progress; Working Together Is Success.' Let's prayerfully agree to work *together* for the glory of God. Find out more by visiting **waverleyabbey.org** or write to me: **micha@edwj.org**

SOMETHING TO CONSIDER: What reservations do you have about expressing God's glory within your worlds?

AN ACTION TO TAKE: Consider if you can take one or all of the three decisions above.

A PRAYER TO MAKE: 'Lord, I am Your servant and agree to live for You and serve You according to Your will.'

Beyond Imagination

We are not fighting against flesh-and-blood enemies, but against evil rulers and authorities of the unseen world. Ephesians 6:12

In our technological age of reason, such verses can strike a discordant note. Am I expected to believe in a world beyond the one I experience with my mind? My answer is a definite yes.

I do not expect us to conjure up images of mythological beasts, for they remain the products of our imagination. I do expect that we accept that Jesus came from beyond our time/space world and returned to it at His ascension. This understanding lays the foundation for our commitment to prayer. We will never resolve the problem of evil through human solutions alone, no matter how sophisticated. There remains a faultline throughout history which once threatened to terminate history itself. Through the incarnate life, death and resurrection of Jesus, its total destructive powers were disarmed.

However, it remains unstable and dangerous. It retains sufficient power to corrupt even the best of us. It's why we face a never ending inner conflict between doing good and doing bad; promoting self or serving everyone's best interests. Many will have enjoyed C. S Lewis', *Chronicles of Narnia*. Our common mistake is to conclude they were myths. Lewis was presenting clearly the reality of an unseen struggle in which warfare is real and control over truth is strongly contested.

The devil remains on the prowl and Scripture constantly reminds us that we are his prey. We must not fall into a false sense of optimism that all is well in the world. Rather we need to heed God's call to arms.

This warfare remains a reality in our own world. And we, Paul explains, are on the frontline of this ceaseless warfare. Our battles are not fiction; our battles are in maintaining faith in God in a battle with fundamentalist rationality.

SOMETHING TO CONSIDER: How have you experienced this hidden war that surrounds us all?

AN ACTION TO TAKE: Read Ephesians 6:10–18 and consider where you are vulnerable to attack.

A PRAYER TO MAKE: 'Lord, help me to be alert to the attacks of the enemy all aimed at damaging my faith in Jesus.'

TUESDAY 23 MARCH

Armour of God

Put on all God's armour so that you will be able to stand firm against all strategies of the devil. Ephesians 6:12

Armour appears an antiquated word. We think of medieval knights riding to war, on horseback. In reality the word is still current as in the body armour police wear, offering them protection against assault.

Paul invites us to take our discipleship seriously. The devil has one purpose which is to destabilise and misdirect us from our chosen goal: to follow Jesus. It's the reason we are so easily distracted from our good intentions to pray. Here we enter the shallows of the warfare to which we are called by God.

Over my many years driving, I've not had many accidents. The few I've had are all down to my being distracted. I wasn't paying full attention to my situation. So I scraped a gate, reversed into a tree stump and bumped a stationary vehicle in front of me. No personal damage, but financial costs that I had to meet. As in everything, there are real consequences to being distracted. Yet the principle stands. It's why Peter warns us to be vigilant at all times.[2] In choosing to follow Jesus we've taken sides and have a formidable foe before us. Yet, Jesus' promise stands firm; 'Here on earth you will have many trials and sorrows. But take heart, because I have overcome the world'.[3]

God's provision is a carefully crafted suit of armour that will ensure we withstand all assaults mounted against us. It may sound frightening, for all warfare is unpleasant. However, much as in Narnia, we are commissioned to pray and work for God's Kingdom to come on earth.

As Paul reminded Timothy, we are soldiers of Christ.[4] We have enlisted and are subject to God's authority in our lives. Our weapons are those of love and compassion; our commission to restore rather than take lives.

SOMETHING TO CONSIDER: Do you think of yourself as a soldier on the frontline of God's mission?

AN ACTION TO TAKE: Learn to recognise distractions that interrupt your intention to pray and serve.

A PRAYER TO MAKE: 'Lord, make me aware of the distractions that direct me away from You, so I might press on and serve You in Your mission.'

[2] 1 Peter 5:8; [3] John 16:33. See also Acts 14:21-22;
[4] 2 Timothy 2:1-7

Be Prepared

Therefore, put on every piece of God's armour so you will be able to resist the enemy in the time of evil. Then after the battle you will still be standing firm. Ephesians 6:13

It's essential that when we get dressed for a job we put on all that we need to protect ourselves. When I first ventured into using a chainsaw I discovered that cut resistant trousers, a helmet, visor, boots and cut resistant gloves were recommended. Chainsaws have a habit of kicking back and injuring the user if they hit a knot in the branch.

It would be all too easy to wield the chainsaw, yet end up injuring myself because I didn't have all the correct clothing. In doing so, I'd have basically removed myself from the frontline. So it is with the armour of God. Every piece is carefully designed and necessary for our protection as we engage in our spiritual warfare.

My assumption that I just needed a chainsaw to get the job done was changed as I listened to someone who had experience on their side. One of the advantages of having Scripture is that we can draw upon the experience of men such as Paul. Pioneers in their day who have left a rich deposit for our benefit. Scripture is God's critical instruction for the Christian way.

Of course we have to find armour that fits us and is appropriate for the task at hand. When David took on Goliath, King Saul offered him his armour for protection. This would have been the very best money could buy. Yet, David struggled to get it on. It wasn't tailormade for him. His natural fighting talent, learnt as a shepherd protecting his flocks, relied on speed of movement and the swift, fluid action of his catapult arm.[5]

The result may well have gone the other way had David assumed that armour alone, however effective, would keep him safe. We need to be aware of both the nature of the warfare we are engaging with and dress appropriately, whilst ensuring we put on every piece of armour God recommends.

SOMETHING TO CONSIDER: Have you been fighting in the most suitable armour?

AN ACTION TO TAKE: Start prayerfully putting on each piece of God's armour at the start of every day.

A PRAYER TO MAKE: 'Lord, help me to put on the armour of God that is made specifically for me in the battles I face.'

[5] 1 Samuel 17:32-40

THURSDAY 25 MARCH

Stand Strong

Stand your ground, putting on the belt of truth and the body armour of God's righteousness. Ephesians 6:14

The greatest challenge in my Christian life are the three words, 'Stand your ground'. Both in keeping my faith among my peers and acting with integrity, I confess to having lost ground to the devil more times than I like to admit. Often it's simply a nudge in the wrong direction. Suddenly I'm sliding down a bank of my own confusion ending up in a heap of humiliation. Of course I can climb back. But it takes time, commitment and effort. Often I've just wallowed in self pity.

Temptation wants to undermine us the moment it interrupts our thoughts. Once we agree to entertain it, there's that nudge and now we're on the slippery slope. God's armour is what we need to face the enemy and hold our ground. Note, there's no armour for our backs.

So, we begin with the belt of truth. Increasing numbers of studies describe 'truth decay'. In our public life, in marketing and across our media, fact checking has become essential. We've lost confidence in what we're told. As disciples, Truth first won our hearts and laid the solid foundation for our Christian life. Without truth we lose trust. Once trust is lost, life's GPS system crashes. Everyone does what's right in their own eyes.

Next put on the breastplate of righteousness. God demands that we walk in the light. That means no secrets! I commend the daily practice of Examen: closing out my day by reflecting on what I did well and where I let myself and God down. Repentance and forgiveness are the keys to living in God's light. We do well to guard our heart. When we've felt betrayed, our confidence collapses and we are subject to feelings of rage and bitterness. When we are economical with the truth, we damage our own conscience.

God can equip us to live life well and enjoy peace within. That's why we need to put on God's armour.

SOMETHING TO CONSIDER: How do you rate your own performance when it comes to 'truth decay'?

AN ACTION TO TAKE: Consider a simple Examen at the end of your day. Write to **micha.jazz@edwj.org** for a copy of what he uses.

A PRAYER TO MAKE: 'Lord, may I reject temptation the moment it interrupts my thoughts. May I live in the light and practice truth telling everywhere.'

Simply Church

– New Edition

By Sim Dendy

In light of all the changes that churches have faced in the last year, we're releasing a new edition of Simply Church, in which Sim has written a chapter all about being agile in response to difficult situations.

From his experience of both attending and leading churches, Sim Dendy asks some key questions about how we 'do' church, just in case there's something we could be doing differently.

Sim looks at the church as being somewhere we can **encounter** God, **gather** together with other believers, **grow** in our faith and knowledge of God's Word, and therefore **influence** the world around us – even if we can't always do all this face-to-face. While church systems are really important, nothing should eclipse the church's purpose in being God's great hope for the world.

Be encouraged as you discover just how simple church can be: how we can get connected, grow stronger, manage our resources and really make a difference.

To find out more and to purchase, visit waverleyabbeyresources.org/product/simply-church

SUNDAY 28 MARCH

Palm Sunday

Say to Daughter Zion 'See, your king comes to you, gentle and riding on a donkey, and on a colt, the foal of a donkey.' Matthew 21:5

Today is Palm Sunday. It marks the start of Jesus' journey to the Cross. Exuberant celebrations greet His arrival into Jerusalem only to give way to angry demands for his execution. So often the distance between exultation and despair is wafer thin.

All too easily Jesus might have been persuaded by the rapturous welcome that ushered him into the city. Just maybe His message had been grasped and these were indeed committed followers. Yet, Jesus never let His guard drop. He knew that praise and celebration too often lack the power to endure rigorous testing.

This was indeed a time for Jesus to remind Himself of His mission. Distractions must be avoided at all costs. In everything God has a purpose. In choosing to follow Jesus we must consider if we have the resilience to stay the distance. Time would reveal none of His twelve most devoted disciples could withstand the demands of faithfulness.

Warfare is real and presents each one of us with questions. As in all of life it's sensible to know where my stress points lie. These are where I am most likely to fracture under pressure. Knowing oneself is critical to any fight we are drawn into. When I know myself, strengths and weaknesses, I am better positioned to emerge successful from life's struggles.

Jesus knew His mission; His Father, the sole source of His strength; and the importance of prayer and God's Word in maintaining an appropriate perspective. In following Jesus we too must know when to celebrate and when to endure. Our mission to love and serve God in all things. Our anchor and our compass God's living Word, the Bible. Prayer, our source of strength and encounter with the Truth.

SOMETHING TO CONSIDER: How are you serving God? How confident are you in Scripture? Is prayer the source of your enduring strength?

AN ACTION TO TAKE: Order a copy of *Bouncing Forward*, where Patrick Regan explores building resilience for life's many challenges.
Visit **edwj.org/ma21-28mar**

A PRAYER TO MAKE: 'Lord, may Your Word provide a lamp for my feet and a light on my path.'

Self-Absorbed

As Jesus approached Jerusalem and saw the city, he wept over it and said, 'If you, even you, had only known on this day what would bring you peace – but now it is hidden from your eyes. Luke 19:41–42

Today we begin our walk with Jesus towards His crucifixion. Following his triumphal entry into the city, whose name means 'foundation of peace', Jesus laments the upcoming rebellion of the city and its people. Only faith in Christ can bring true peace; in rejecting Jesus we create conflict and chaos.

The degree to which Jesus loves us is evident in the tears He shed over the city. Not tears about His own fate, but tears for others. The nature of God is always to yearn for the best interest of others. Life may offer us a bumpy ride, yet God wants to accompany us over the bumps.

When I've faced personal loss and disappointment I quickly become self-absorbed. 'Why me!', I exclaim. It seems so unfair. Yet, if I paused long enough to draw the lens back and look more closely at my neighbourhood, I'd discover individuals facing huge and unwelcome challenges. Indeed, partly because of my age, I see so many friends battling issues of ill health, redundancy or grief. Jesus continues to prophesy Jerusalem's destruction. If we fail to turn to God then our destruction is the consequence. The whole drama of this week is the revelation that despite our inability to save ourselves, we have been given a Saviour. One who knows us inside out, yet still loves us entirely.

Much of my life I've chased acceptance and affirmation, both aspects of love. I've attempted to disguise my less attractive traits in that pursuit. Yet, I've let myself down all too often and when my attempts to win love fail, I readily blame others, not myself. Like Jerusalem I remained blind for too long, failing to acknowledge, and then discover, true peace is found in God alone.

SOMETHING TO CONSIDER: Are you able to discover God as you navigate bumps along life's path?

AN ACTION TO TAKE: Consider one such painful bump you have faced, or are now experiencing. What might you learn that can be of value not just to yourself, but to others in similar circumstances?

A PRAYER TO MAKE: 'Lord, open my eyes so that I can find you in the difficult challenges life presents me with.'

TUESDAY 30 MARCH

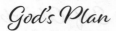

God's Plan

> **Jesus entered the temple courts and drove out all who were buying and selling there. He overturned the tables of the money-changers and the benches of those selling doves.** Matthew 21:12

This is an interesting story in the Scripture. Some assume Jesus was angry, yet the Bible never says that He was. But why does he feel the necessity to overturn tables and expel the money changers? The issue is most likely that Jewish coins were mixed with the Roman coins. The latter bore the image of Caesar, and Jesus made a clear distinction about giving to Caesar, or the world system, what it is owed whilst giving to God what is owed to Him.[8]

Jesus makes it clear that the Temple is a house of prayer, as declared by Isaiah.[9] There is a distinction made between God and the world. Jesus is demonstrating that there is much that will distract us from God in the opportunities and activities life affords. We must have an eye to remain focussed upon God.

Of course we know that we are indeed today's temples of the Holy Spirit.[10] We are to ensure that our outward and visible actions together with our inner and hidden thoughts are pure. There's always a danger that, like the Pharisees, we can clean up our act on the outside, whilst refusing to address the inner world of our natural appetites.

As temples of the Holy Spirit we are sources of continuous prayer wherever we go. St. Paul reminds us in his letter to the Thessalonians, we are to pray without ceasing.[11] So in short we have a responsibility to ensure we are fit for the purpose of prayer and service as God intends.

I must ask myself in everything I think and do, am I responding to Jesus' invitation to follow Him? I recognise it is all too easily to attempt great things for God, yet to compromise on the faith that alone can give them value and virtue.

SOMETHING TO CONSIDER: Review what you do and why you do it. Consider if this is how God intends you to live as a temple of the Holy Spirit.

AN ACTION TO TAKE: Read Dave Smith's *God's Plan for Your Wellbeing* our 50 day guide to improve your daily life rhythm. Visit **edwj.org/ma21-30mar**

A PRAYER TO MAKE: 'Lord, may my life act as a prayer for the nations.'

[8]Mark 12:17; [9]Isaiah 56:7; [10]1 Corinthians 6:12-20;
[11]1 Thessalonians 5:17

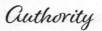 *Authority*

Jesus entered the temple courts, and, while he was teaching, the chief priests and the elders of the people came to him. 'By what authority are you doing these things?' they asked. 'And who gave you this authority?' Matthew 21:23

The word 'authority' raises the issue of permission. Buried within it is the word 'author', the one who creates the narrative. In our democratic societies we have become accustomed to looking to the people to permission our politicians through an election. Yet, who gives Jesus His permission to make the promises He does?

This is critical for us. For if Jesus' authority is invalid, we can have little to no confidence in God's promises. Jesus' authority is both given and taken. We understand God to be both first cause and final end. There is nothing outside of God. Were there to be such a 'thing', God would be subject to its influence. Immediately God's omnipotence, God's unlimited power, would come into question.

Jesus being present at the creation of everything has all authority by virtue of being God. Yet, in His incarnation, as both God and man, Jesus voluntarily subjects Himself to God's authority. As the writer to the Hebrews writes, Jesus submitted as God's son to His Father's discipline.[12] Earlier that same writer refers to Jesus as the 'author of our faith'.[13]

When Jesus answers the chief priests with a question, it immediately causes them to hesitate. For they want to exploit a false authority to establish their personal agenda. They have no authority, only that which they have manufactured. Jesus, however, carries the full authority of heaven, and we are invited to both live under that authority and to exercise it through the Holy Spirit in our lives. In short we are to live in the confidence that we are co-heirs with Christ, and that means we share both in Christ's sufferings and in Christ's triumphs.[14]

SOMETHING TO CONSIDER: How do you exercise God's authority in your life in service and in resisting temptation?

AN ACTION TO TAKE: Read Hebrews 12 in the Bible and decide where your personal walk of faith might be improved.

A PRAYER TO MAKE: 'Lord, thank You that You are the author and finisher of my faith. May I walk in Your footsteps hour by hour and day by day.'

[12]Hebrews 12:3-11; [13]Hebrews 12:1-2;
[14]Romans 8:1-17

THURSDAY 1 APRIL

Abandonment

> **Jesus said, 'The Son of Man will go just as it is written about him. But woe to that man who betrays the Son of Man! It would be better for him if he had not been born.'** Matthew 26:24

Today is the day of Jesus' betrayal. He is deliberately exposed to harm through a trusted friend's actions.[15] There is perhaps no more bitter a pill to swallow than a friend's disloyalty. Our safe space is destroyed and we must face unexpected consequences. We are ill prepared and feel the pain deep within. My wife Jayne experienced abandonment by her then-husband when she was seven months pregnant. The bitterness of that occasion has left its grubby fingerprints impressed upon her life. Forgiveness is extended, yet the sharp pain of rejection remains. We are created for relationship – hence our friendship with God. So it is deeply distressing when a friendship is broken. There is seldom an opportunity to process the loss with the one who betrays us. We are left to conjecture on the reasons why and instinctively become suspicious of all relationships. Jesus acknowledges the sanctity of honesty and loyalty even as He condemns Judas' action. It's not Judas, but the choice Judas takes and acts upon. Each of us is subject to thoughts both good and bad. In themselves these must be managed. Yet, once acted upon they have impacts that may reach well beyond anything we imagined. Wholesome relationships are the currency of God's Kingdom. We are to love others to the same degree that we love ourselves.[16] God forgives us to the degree that we forgive others.[17] This equally applies to our relationship with God. This is unique and precious and whilst we shall make mistakes, as St. Peter clearly illustrates, there is a way back to God through acknowledgement and forgiveness. However, when we fail to address the break, we choose to stand beyond God's reach.

SOMETHING TO CONSIDER: Are there friendships that have ended badly either by you or by another? Consider what prayer and action you can take to break down the remaining walls of hostility between you.[18]

AN ACTION TO TAKE: If you are asking yourself, 'What do I do when I can't forgive? Is reconciliation always possible? Does God condemn me? How can I forgive myself?', then read *Insight into Forgiveness*. Visit **edwj.org/ma21-1apr**

A PRAYER TO MAKE: 'Lord, help me to break down those walls of hostility that imprison me, by Your grace and forgiveness.'

[15]Matthew 26:14-16; [16]Mark 12:30-31;
[17]Matthew 6:12; [18]Ephesians 1:14-18

Crucifixion

And when Jesus had cried out again in a loud voice, he gave up his spirit. Matthew 27:50

We are familiar with Jesus' crucifixion, yet we must never grow comfortable with it. Whilst it grants humanity the opportunity for personal encounter with God, the price of forgiveness, both to God and to all responding to God's offer, weighs heavily in the balance.

Scripture is clear, no-one took Jesus' life; He voluntarily gave it up in an act of redemption for all who choose to bow the knee and accept forgiveness.[19] This was not an execution that the authorities could quietly action on a forlorn hill outside Jerusalem. Jesus cried out in a loud voice, and all of creation responded with a series of unexpected natural phenomena.[20] The whole world was adjusting to a new order, the rhythm of the Kingdom of God arriving.

This event, intended to anonymise Jesus to a footnote in history, only fostered the dawning of a global movement still growing 2000 years after it was recorded. Murdered amongst Jerusalem's rubbish, this man demonstrates He is Messiah, the rescuer of humanity, who continues to seek and find us amongst the rubbish that often constitutes our own lives. Today, this same Jesus is alive – it's Friday but Sunday's coming – and voluntarily meets us with a message of hope in the rubbish that clutters up our own lives. He alone holds the power to guide us to freedom from that rubbish. This is the miracle of the cross.

The choice is simple. Jesus surrendered to death so we might enjoy friendship with God. Am I willing to surrender myself to God daily? Not only when the sun shines, but also when the storm clouds gather. 'Come follow me', is a simple invitation. But learning to live every day with Jesus challenges me to my core. Am I up for the challenge?

SOMETHING TO CONSIDER: Listen to Chris Tomlin's *Love Ran Red* on YouTube as an act of worship (**edwj.org/ma21-2apr**).

AN ACTION TO TAKE: Consider what rubbish has built up in your life which you'd like to be rid of. Invite Jesus to carry it away and recommit to learning to live every day with Jesus.

A PRAYER TO MAKE: 'Lord, I believe. Help my unbelief.'

[19]John 10:18; [20]Matthew 27:51-54

SATURDAY 3 APRIL

Burial

He was accompanied by Nicodemus, the man who earlier had visited Jesus at night. Nicodemus brought a mixture of myrrh and aloes, about thirty-five kilograms. John 19:39

Taken from the cross and prepared for burial, Jesus is laid to rest in a stranger's tomb. Despised by those who killed him, after death He is treated with dignity and respect by His friends. Here, emerging from the shadows not for the first time, we meet Nicodemus again. His initial questions with which we started this edition of *Every Day with Jesus* self evidently answered sufficiently for him to have become a follower. He is here, at quite some personal risk, to play his part in honouring Jesus. Even in death Jesus has the power to draw people to himself.

This is a time of great silence. The sabbath is arriving. The burial must be completed speedily. The commotion surrounding the crucifixion has dispersed with the crowd. Now just a few friends work quietly to do what they can for their friend's corpse. Each season between tasting failure and finding fresh faith is marked by silence. Our energy of complaint and fear has been expended. Our words apparently falling empty to the ground. Exhausted both by fear and endeavour, we have expended our emotional ardour. Now we must wait with the uncertainty of what tomorrow might bring. Yet, despite our grief, fear and disappointment, so much more may be taking place than we are conscious of. This was true on the eve of the Sabbath. Little did these faithful mourners know that their worst fears would not be realised and that in fact God had this in hand. We are reminded that we are always called to live by faith, not sight. Faith in God's promise, even as circumstances appear to present a very different story. For, 'faith is confidence in what we hope for and assurance about what we do not see'.[21]

SOMETHING TO CONSIDER: Learning to maintain confidence in God in the silence is a key part of our spiritual formation.

AN ACTION TO TAKE: Finding faith in challenging circumstances can prove tough. Read *Shattered* by Rachel and Tim Wright, forty readings looking at life's many twists and turns, **edwj.org/ma21-3apr**

A PRAYER TO MAKE: 'Lord, help me to remain faithful during periods of uncertainty and fear.'

[21] Hebrews 11:1

Insight

Helping you and
helping others

Mental health is one of the big topics right now and it's extremely important to God. Whether you are struggling, or you're supporting someone else, we've got a range of resources that will help you.

Our Insight range includes books, devotionals and online courses. We are passionate about people's wellbeing, and so we cover topics that many people struggle with but that are often overlooked, feared or misunderstood. We look at real-life examples, theory and biblical wisdom, so that you can take steps forward.

An insight into
anxiety

Clare Blake and Chris Ledger

CWR
WAVERLEY ABBEY INSIGHT SERIES

An insight into
shame

Heather Churchill and Claire Muste

CWR
WAVERLEY ABBEY INSIGHT SERIES

An insight into
depression

Wendy Bray and Chris Ledger

CWR
WAVERLEY ABBEY INSIGHT SERIES

Visit **waverleyabbeyresources.org/insight** to find out more

SUNDAY 4 APRIL

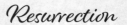
Resurrection

> **Early on the first day of the week, while it was still dark, Mary Magdalene went to the tomb and saw that the stone had been removed from the entrance.** John 20:1

Imagine the scene. There is a deep calm all around. It's early, the day hardly started. The turbulent events of Holy Week have passed. I recall my own childhood when Sunday was a day of rest, and the quiet so loud you could almost hear it.

Mary makes her way to Jesus' tomb to pay her respects. She pauses, shocked at what greets her. Jesus' tomb disturbed with the stone sealing its entrance rolled away. Her quiet contemplation is shattered at the thought that someone has stolen Jesus' body. Her stillness turns to anguished concern and she runs off in search of the disciples.

Mary's humanity reflects our own. Our instinct is usually to fear the worst. A family member is late home and we assume a traffic accident or worse. I often ask myself why it is that we fear the worst rather than believe for the best? It appears that no matter how much we listen to God, the challenge is in recalling God's Word in each specific situation. Jesus carefully taught His followers about His death and resurrection. Yet, whilst they had heard His words they'd failed to understand their meaning. Listening to learn so that we might live the Christian life lies at the heart of our spiritual formation.

When we can't make sense of something, it's easier to doubt, even deny, what we don't understand. Understanding actually means to 'stand among'. We must choose if we believe through the lens of logic or intellect or our conviction that God's word is true. This then demands learning to live by sightless faith as surely as a blind person relies upon their guide dog. To stand among God's Word and God's people.

SOMETHING TO CONSIDER: Mary feared the worst. What fears and anxieties do you confront at present?

AN ACTION TO TAKE: Fear and anxiety rob us of our peace. Identify someone you trust who you are able to share your anxieties with. They may not have the answer, but they can listen to you, perhaps pray with you. A problem shared eases the weight we carry.

A PRAYER TO MAKE: 'Lord, thank You that You rose from the dead, and are alive today and forever.'

Despondency

She turned towards him and cried out in Aramaic, 'Rabboni!' (which means 'Teacher'). John 20:16

I have discovered that Jesus often surprises me. Despondent because of apparently unanswered prayers or engaged in challenging life circumstances, I assume that Jesus is nowhere to be found. My initial thoughts are to abandon my confidence in Christ and look to my own resources to get me out of a difficult spot.

Of course, logically I know that God is always with me, yet I can still feel so completely alone. I'm insufficient to deliver myself from my challenge. Discovering that Katey, my first wife, and I were unable to have children, followed by her MS diagnosis, left me drowning in my own inadequacy and fear. Mary, having assumed the worst, that Jesus' body has been stolen, fails to recognise Him. Again she assumes this must be the gardener. She pleads for information. At least she is praying to the right person! Then she hears a familiar voice. All anxiety drains from her being in the surprise at meeting her risen Lord. This is her teacher indeed, the one who gave her knowledge of life. In this amazing moment she makes an essential discovery: that living the truth she has learnt involves her activating her will and her choice.

Too often I blame God for my circumstances. Yet, the truth of all that I know about God is to enable me to live at peace within the limitations of every circumstance. Christianity is not some charmed journey leading me to heaven. It is practical and robust, a faith based approach to overcoming life's difficulties by God's grace and through applying God's Word. Only as I put legs on my faith and walk it out in the world in which I find myself does it have an authenticity. Only then is it a witness to my risen Lord and ever present teacher.

SOMETHING TO CONSIDER: How do you discern the voice of God in your life circumstances?

AN ACTION TO TAKE: Read Selwyn Hughes' *Christ Empowered Living*, a practical approach to living God's Word in everyday life. Visit **edwj.org/ma21-5apr**

A PRAYER TO MAKE: 'Lord, thank You that You are present in the fiercest of storms, even when I cannot find You.'

TUESDAY 6 APRIL

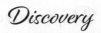
Discovery

> **Finally the other disciple (John), who had reached the tomb first, also went inside. He saw and believed.** John 20:8

It's said that 'seeing is believing'. The inexplicable must be seen for what others say can't be trusted. We need tangible proof. Yet here Peter and John reach the tomb and believe on the basis of what they can't see, Jesus' body. There is the evidence of the carefully folded shroud, but it required faith to accept Jesus is risen.

What's true for the disciples is true for us. I was first drawn to Jesus as someone described Jesus. Yet, only when I chose to commit my life to the truth I hoped might prove genuine did I discover Christ is real. I came to encounter God daily in my life experiences.

I still lose sight of God and struggle to entrust my total welfare to God. Yet, in my struggle to trust I cannot escape the experience that I've encountered and know God personally. Initially it was tough. My family thought I was passing through a 'religious phase'. Many friends disagreed with me, some ending our friendship because 'I'd got religion'.

The mystery remains for Jesus had now transcended the physical to become both the physical and the intangible. This is why faith is so challenging both to grasp and to practice. For now, the incarnate Jesus can only be found with eyes of faith. With His resurrection, God's redemptive plan locks into place. In a moment these two disciples saw the coming together of all of human history and the fulfillment of the Law and the Prophets. As such we, the Church, are invited to live in our physical world but always with a sense of the spiritual, the now yet unseen, presence of God. The tomb's forever empty, yet Christ is forever present with us.

SOMETHING TO CONSIDER: Today, follow the disciples into the empty tomb and reflect upon the reality of God when you can find no tangible evidence for such a reality.

AN ACTION TO TAKE: In the reality of everyday living, with its hustle and bustle, seek Christ's presence with the eyes of faith.

A PRAYER TO MAKE: 'Lord, thank You that You are risen from the dead and so present in all of life and available to me wherever I am and whatever I face.'

On the evening of that first day of the week, when the disciples were together, with the doors locked for fear of the Jewish leaders, Jesus came and stood among them and said, 'Peace be with you!' John 20:19

When confronted by our fear we often find comfort in the companionship of friends. We are made for relationships, and perhaps the hardest test to endure is being robbed of those we love and trust. Last October, having lived separated from her family for seven months, my mum succumbed to her 95 years and died. I am left wondering, if normal visitation had been allowed whether she might have continued longer? For her sake, I don't regret her passing into her well-earned eternal rest. Yet, as I gaze upon the most wonderful photograph of her smiling face, which I had the presence of mind to snap the last time I saw her fit and able the day before lockdown, I'm aware how I miss her. What if she craved my company through that long season of isolation? I am not alone here, for many endured such experiences, yet it reminds me of the importance of presence. Here the disciples gather together, lock themselves away for fear of the authorities. They are, after all, Jesus' accomplices! And yet, now joined through their mutual fear, they encounter the risen Jesus. He immediately calms their fears by granting them God's peace. And here's the joy of living every day with Jesus. Not one of us can predict the future, yet we can always encounter the risen Christ just as those first disciples did. The same risen Christ is our companion today.

When I was allowed, only on very strict and limited conditions, to visit mum as she lay waiting for God's summon home, I held her hand and stroked her cheek whilst I prayed. I thanked her, encouraged her that all her family were well and entrusted her to God's care. Alone together in that room, I knew our hearts were joined and the presence of God joined us. It was a holy moment, for Christ is risen to meet, greet and accompany us every step of our life.

SOMETHING TO CONSIDER: 'Jesus! the name that charms our fears, That bids our sorrows cease; 'Tis music in the sinner's ears, 'Tis life, and health, and peace.' Reflect on these words of Charles Wesley.

AN ACTION TO TAKE: Take your real fears to friends who can encourage you through prayer and together discover the peace of God that passes all understanding.[22]

A PRAYER TO MAKE: 'Lord of peace, please give me peace at all times and in every way.'

[22] Philippians 4:7

THURSDAY 8 APRIL

Peace

> **Again Jesus said, 'Peace be with you! As the Father has sent me, I am sending you.' And with that he breathed on them and said, 'Receive the Holy Spirit.** John 20:21-22

For a second time Jesus speaks peace over the disciples. When something is repeated in scripture, it is a clear assurance of its truth. We see this throughout the psalms, and it strengthens faith. This peace is confirmed by the gift of the Holy Spirit. This third person of the Trinity, who is God, resides within us to lead us into all truth.[23]

It has taken me years to enter into the peace that Jesus promised. Or, more accurately, to become familiar and comfortable with the reality that my life is secure in God's hands. Knowing God's peace and living in God's peace often proved mutually exclusive. I still waver and need to make choices about my faith commitment. When I was a youth worker I presented faith with a trust exercise. I'd ask someone if they were confident I'd catch them if they fell backwards. Getting their assent was't hard. But when testing their confidence it was often different. I'd stand behind them and ask them to fall backwards on the count of three. They would start to lean backwards, yet often, at the point of no return, they'd put one leg back to steady themselves. A few would trust in my promise and they came to rest safely in my arms and I pushed them back into an upright position.

Peace is not about living a comfortable life. It's the learning that, no matter what I face, I can confidently fall backwards into the trustworthy arms of God. Jesus commissions his disciples to live as he has lived, in total devotion and confidence in God. He breathes the Holy Spirit on them. Their next encounter with the Spirit is at Pentecost. This second encounter offers them the full assurance that God is indeed with them to the end of the age, and so they move beyond fear and boldly live life in God's active service.

SOMETHING TO CONSIDER: Am I confident allowing myself to fall back into God's arms?[24]

AN ACTION TO TAKE: Read *Cover to Cover: The Uniqueness of our Faith* to discover how to live confident in God's promises. Visit, **edwj.org/ma21-8apr**

A PRAYER TO MAKE: 'Lord, breath Your spirit afresh on me today as I live in Your peace and serve You in mission.'

[23]John 16:13; [24]Deuteronomy 33:27

Bouncing Forward

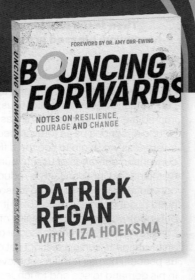

FOREWORD BY DR. AMY ORR-EWING

BOUNCING FORWARDS

NOTES ON RESILIENCE, COURAGE AND CHANGE

PATRICK REGAN
WITH LIZA HOEKSMA

Suffering, trauma, anxiety, grief – so many of us experience these. Given all that has gone on over the past year, it's likely that we've all experienced a struggle or major set-back to some degree recently. So where do we go from there?

In this new, relatable book from Patrick Regan, discover what it looks like to face these things as a Christian.

Bouncing Forward will help you understand what true resilience really is, and how it goes beyond bouncing back. By looking at stories, words of wisdom and personal insights from Patrick, you'll be able to understand how the times when you may feel you're going backwards can actually springboard you forward. Nothing you go through is ever wasted.

'I want to bounce forward, demonstrating emotional agility when my feelings are threatening to overwhelm me.'

– Patrick Regan

Discover the change that the idea of bouncing forward can make for you and your situation. Order today at
waverleyabbeyresources.org/product/bouncing-forward

Patrick Regan is CEO of Kintsugi Hope, which he founded with his wife, Diane. His recent books include Honesty Over Silence (Waverley Abbey Resources), which seeks to open up conversations around topics that some find difficult.

FRIDAY 9 APRIL

Acknowledgement

> **Then Jesus told him, 'Because you have seen me, you have believed; blessed are those who have not seen and yet have believed.'** John 20:29

Thomas is forever associated with doubt, when in fact he was full of belief. He did demand to place his finger in the wounds to establish this was really Jesus, but when he encountered Christ he immediately acknowledged him as Lord and God.[25]

Jung describes us as forever 'becoming'.* As we grow in human awareness we begin to see the differences between what social convention demands of us and our preferences. Our faith is challenged. All too easily Christian faith is reduced to little more than a social convention. Whilst searching for something to meet my inner spiritual need ('...our heart is restless until it finds its rest in you' declared Augustine of Hippo) we can miss the reality of God completely. Jesus can never be constrained by convention, social or religious. His whole life message is an invitation to serve a distinct set of Kingdom values. These alone offer us peace. Thomas remains unmoved by his fellow disciples' stories. Yet, in his demand to see and touch Jesus' wounds he reveals his desire for truth. Finding this truth demands he suspend rationality and embrace the reality of resurrection. Thomas' eyes needed opening. For most of us life is framed when young. Reason insists that nothing is true until established as measurable fact. This can never lead us into God's presence. For love, be it human or divine, lies beyond objective measures. It is a conviction born of encounter and experience. God lies beyond formulation, yet never outside of friendship. In our risk averse age, where even 'friendship' is easily reduced to personal advantage, any conviction based upon abstracts, such as encounter, requires courage. This is the courage Thomas demonstrates. Faith remains a courageous walk every day.

SOMETHING TO CONSIDER: How would you describe your latest encounter with God?

AN ACTION TO TAKE: Faith begins in encounter. What do you believe you are withholding from God? Why is it so hard to surrender?

A PRAYER TO MAKE: 'Lord, help me to find confidence that nothing is impossible with You.'

[25] John 20:24-28
*Delden Anne McNeedy, *Becoming* (Fisher-King, 2010)

Do You Love Me?

The third time he said to him, 'Simon son of John, do you love me?' Peter was hurt because Jesus asked him the third time, 'Do you love me?' He said, 'Lord, you know all things; you know that I love you.' Jesus said, 'Feed my sheep.' John 21:17

Grace is the remarkable gift we discover in Jesus. Peter, so confident in his faith, stumbled when denying Jesus at his arrest. Now, embarrassed by his betrayal, he returns to fishing, his hopes dashed, his spirit broken. However, the great news is that his friends stuck with him. We live in a time when many are aware of their fragility. Covid-19 reminds us how impotent we are when confronted by a global pandemic. Our knowledge and sophistication hold no answer for this deadly virus. It's often new experiences that test our confidence in God. When my wife Katey was diagnosed with progressive MS, a disease that took her life eighteen years later, I fell apart. A Christian leader, platform preacher and evangelist, I had no answers for our situation. A problem solver with a challenge beyond my competence. With no resources from upbringing, education or experience, I imploded and questioned God's relevance. I behaved in ways that fell short of what this 'man of God' had so often preached. I was a mess and my self-esteem collapsed. Like Peter I was ashamed and wanted to hide within the anonymity of normality. Yet like Peter, God asked me a simple question; 'do you love me?' I did. My problem was I couldn't believe God loved me and I didn't love myself. But God wasn't disillusioned with me; he never had any illusions to start with. He knew me, loved me, accepted me and embraced me when I cried out to Him the very first time. Long before I had an opportunity to demonstrate my commitment. The remarkable thing about God's love is that it never runs dry. I may choose to absent myself from God, but God is always waiting close by ready to renew and restore our friendship.

SOMETHING TO CONSIDER: Do you feel you have let God down? Are you ready to make up? God is!

AN ACTION TO TAKE: Read John 21 and make notes of what lessons you can take and apply to your own friendship with God.

A PRAYER TO MAKE: 'Lord, You know that I love You. Help to love myself and deepen our friendship.'

SUNDAY 11 APRIL

Belief With Legs

These are written that you may believe that Jesus is the Messiah, the Son of God, and that by believing you may have life in his name. John 20:31

Understanding and belief are different. Belief is the acceptance that something is true without proof. Belief is faith and offers understanding with legs on. Faith carries us somewhere, whilst understanding leaves us motionless. The first disciples understood Jesus as risen, they had tangible evidence, yet they needed the outpouring of the Holy Spirit, born of obedience and prayer, to believe.[26] Indeed belief with legs marked out the Old Testament heroes who had no such encounter with the risen Christ, yet obediently responded to God's word. Noah built an ark in a sunbaked land, whilst Abraham left home for an unknown destination.[27] Encounter with God is less about understanding than putting one's life at God's disposal. It takes courage to live off a promise; yet a promise is all we have. When Jayne entered hospital with Covid-19 in March, she looked back to say goodbye, but I'd already been ushered away. Then her phone was taken from her for fear of infection, placed in a sealed bag and stored. She remembers thinking, 'I may never leave here or see Micha again'. She knew she had a choice. She could be consumed with fear or continue into the unknown with God. After all doesn't God work all things together for good for those who love and are called according to God's purpose?[28] She made her choice, and even as she saw people emerge from behind curtains, intubated on trolleys, she chose to hang her hat on the promises of God. Life or death, everything was in God's hands. 'Fear not, for I am with you', sounded in her spirit and she began a long afternoon of tests.[29] Scripture tells us faith comes by hearing. This is always that still, small voice of God.[30] Without it there will always remain a great disconnect between our understanding and belief.

SOMETHING TO CONSIDER: How do I understand the difference between understanding and belief?

AN ACTION TO TAKE: Purchase a copy of *Bible 60* and discover key turning points in the story of God and His people and the part you can play in God's story today: **edwj.org/ma21-11apr**

A PRAYER TO MAKE: 'Lord, help me to learn how to live by faith and not by sight.'

[26]Acts 2; [27]Hebrews 11; [28] Romans 8:28; [29]Matthew 28:20; [30] 1 Kings 19:11-14

Loving God

Yet you, Lord, are our Father. We are the clay, you are the potter; we are all the work of your hand. Isaiah 64:8

This week we shall explore spiritual formation, the heartbeat of discipleship. This is Waverley Abbey's core mission: seeking to live every day with Jesus. It is a journey on which we deliberately and consciously open up our lives for a deeper connectedness with God.

I used to live in Chichester which boasts a fine Cathedral dating from 1075. In 1244, Richard was appointed bishop. An orphan who had prospered in service of God's church, Richard of Chichester was committed to living a life dedicated to God. He also encouraged others through a prayer made famous as one of the leading songs in the musical Godspell. His prayer is simple, 'My Lord Jesus Christ, may I know you more clearly, love you more dearly and follow you more nearly, day by day. Amen'. This is my morning prayer; it is the very essence of spiritual formation. The challenge for each one of us is not what, or in whom, we believe. It is the challenge of living that belief in the circumstances into which life places us. It informs our decisions, determines our outlook and ultimately demonstrates our values. The good news is we are not left on our own. God works with us, just as the potter shapes vessels from nothing more than a ball of clay. Out of our 'nothingness' God can shape a life and a person revealing the glory of God. We also walk alongside other Chrsitians, companions and encouragers along the way.

As Richella Parham says, 'In short, Christian spiritual formation is the process in which believers cooperate with God and one another so that their souls are nourished and their characters are transformed into Christlikeness.'[31]

SOMETHING TO CONSIDER: Reflect upon Richard of Chichester's prayer, 'My Lord Jesus Christ, may I know you more clearly, love you more dearly and follow you more nearly, day by day. Amen.'

AN ACTION TO TAKE: Jesus was tempted and tested but above all He demonstrated a powerful understanding of who He was, and what mattered most to Him. Read *Approaching Jesus* by Cathy Madavan. Visit **edwj.org/ma21-12apr**

A PRAYER TO MAKE: 'Lord, may I know You more clearly, love You more dearly and follow You more nearly, day by day.'

[31] Richella Parham, *'A Spiritual Formation Primer',*
(Renovare, 2013) p.6.

TUESDAY 13 APRIL

My son, pay attention to what I say; turn your ear to my words. Do not let them out of your sight, keep them within your heart for they are life to those who find them and health to one's whole body. Proverbs 4:20–22

The Covid-19 pandemic made us all conscious of our mortal fragility. It spotlights a deep, underlying concern that impacts all of society; health and wellbeing. This is reflected in the huge sums invested by drug companies right through to the pressure placed on GP surgeries as we prepare for the worst and hope for the best. However, we are far more than physical beings. There is within everyone of us a longing for meaning. German has the word 'Sehnsucht' for which there's no English translation. C. S. Lewis used it to express the inconsolable longing that we each feel at times in our lives. It represents our search, often in vain, for something beyond our human capacity. It acts as the border between the physical and the metaphysical. We may set ourselves many goals in life, yet there remain inexpressible longings well beyond the achievement of my goals. Such a longing can create deep dissatisfaction. It is perhaps the intrusion of an awareness that I am incomplete in and of myself. The writer of Proverbs observes that there's a path beyond my comprehension which I must tread to find complete health. This search for inner fulfilment is the substance of spiritual formation. For only God, as revealed in God's word, can satisfy what no other accomplishment can reach. In our pursuit of God there must be an adjustment to our listening and our observing. We are not to be captivated by the material realities our constructive goal setting can achieve for us. Rather, we are to encounter Jesus daily in Scripture and learn to nurture such appetites that draw us closer to God's will and offer satisfaction beyond comparison; that elusive fullness of life Jesus promised His followers.

SOMETHING TO CONSIDER: How would you identify and describe your inner longing? What frustrates you in attempting to realise it?

AN ACTION TO TAKE: "Every time I post to social media, I pray: 'Lord, make me an instrument of your peace.'" Miroslav Wolf.[33] Let's be disciplined in what we say, and why and how we are saying it. I always ask myself, is it true, is it kind, is it necessary?

A PRAYER TO MAKE: 'Lord, I choose to turn my ear to your word and live as You direct.'

[32]John 10:10; [33]https://thequestforagoodlife.com/2020/10/04/becoming-an-instrument-of-peace [accessed 2020/10/24]

Knowing God

For I know the plans I have for you,' declares the Lord, 'plans to prosper you and not to harm you, plans to give you hope and a future. Then you will call on me and come and pray to me, and I will listen to you. You will seek me and find me when you seek me with all your heart. Jeremiah 29:11–13

As a teenager I turned up at university with little idea as to what I wanted in life. No career aspirations and little motivation above personal enjoyment. It was to my great surprise that I encountered Jesus within just a few weeks. More surprising was my willingness to commit to following in His footsteps. I purchased a Bible and was grateful to daily Bible notes to begin my education, coming as I did from an unchurched background. One day, reading in Luke's gospel, I could not stop thinking about Jesus' words on returning from the wilderness; '… to proclaim good news to the poor …to proclaim freedom for the prisoners and recovery of sight for the blind, to set the oppressed free, to proclaim the year of the Lord's favour.'[34] These laid the foundation for my life, although I had no knowledge of that as I first read them. It was the start of a growing understanding that my life, once surrendered to God, was God's to do with as He pleased. Such total surrender is little understood in today's society, where individual rights are argued and fought for passionately. My life was all about setting aside my personal preferences and to take time discovering God and all God has planned for my life. Perhaps understanding is easier as I look back over my life and see how God has put me to work as an evangelist, in working for the incarcerated and running a house of prayer whose purpose is to offer hospitality, hope and healing. Reflecting on Richard of Chichester's prayer, knowing God more clearly only happens as we first surrender daily to God's purpose and so discern God's plans for us. For only as we realise God's plans in our life can we deepen our encounter with God, and God's with us.

SOMETHING TO CONSIDER: Are there scriptures that you have felt compelled to return to many times? What is God saying to you through them?

AN ACTION TO TAKE: Find some time to surrender your life afresh to God whilst praying that you might discover the fullest expression of God's plans for your life.

A PRAYER TO MAKE: 'Lord, daily will I call on You and come and pray to You, and I will listen to You.'

[34]Luke 4:18-19

THURSDAY 15 APRIL

Loving God

And we all, who with unveiled faces contemplate the Lord's glory, are being transformed into his image with ever-increasing glory, which comes from the Lord, who is the Spirit. 2 Corinthians 3:18

L ove is an indefinable quality. We can describe it, yet can never capture its true essence. This can only be encountered through experience. What's more, love is never static. It is either growing or dying. As a wiser and older friend once said to me, 'If I loved my wife today the same as I loved her on the day we got married, my marriage would be on the rocks.' We can never take love for granted, and this includes God's love. Much like the sun God's love is always there, yet there are times when cloud obscures it and the weather surrounding us is distinctly unpleasant. Walking in the Lake District and making an ascent on one of its many fells, it's all too easy to lose one's way as the peak passes in and out of sight. A map to guide one's ascent proves essential. So it is with learning to love God more dearly. It's easy to take God's love for granted and presume on God's promise. Then we grow frustrated when it appears God's abandoned us.

The way to deepen my love for God is to follow the guide, in this case the Bible illuminated by the Holy Spirit. This is the key reason why it's a healthy practice to read and listen to Scripture daily. As I learn more about God's sacrifice and grace, my love for God and desire to serve grows, just as when I take time to get to know my wife, my understanding, appreciation and ability to serve her develops.

There can be no spiritual formation apart from God's Word, for this is the mirror into which we gaze that we might grow closer to God and become more like Jesus in the way we express ourselves in everyday life.

SOMETHING TO CONSIDER: Is reading the Bible like reading a love letter? If not, are there changes you need to make in your approach to Scripture?

AN ACTION TO TAKE: Encounter God afresh as Anne Le Tissier explores how being consistently open to God will release us to fulfil our God-given potential and enable us to experience the fullness of the Spirit in our everyday life.
Visit **edwj.org/ma21-15apr**

A PRAYER TO MAKE: 'Lord, as I gaze upon Your face may I be transformed daily into Your life and realise my purpose.'

Revival Requires Prayer!

Revival is to bring something back to life. As the church of Jesus Christ we have the opportunity to seek God and live the God-life. It is as we turn to Christ and give ourselves to prayer and dedicate our lives to living by God's instructions that we issue an invitation for the Spirit to revive us, and through us, the world. As Waverley Abbey, we are committed to praying for such a fresh visitation of God's Spirit.

Prayer is choosing to stand face to face with God. We shall explore the nature of prayer and how we might pray simply yet in sincerity. We shall consider the five frameworks for prayer and learn how we might give ourselves to this essential activity that ensures that God's will is done on earth. It is at the very heart of all Jesus taught us.

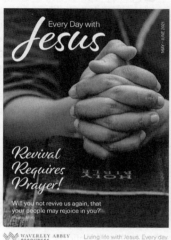

Also available as eBook/eSubscription

FRIDAY 16 APRIL

Following God

> **Walk in obedience to all that the Lord your God has commanded you, so that you may live and prosper and prolong your days in the land that you will possess.** Deuteronomy 5:33

Growing up I was of the opinion that God was something of a spoil sport. I assumed that God was a cosmic police chief issuing a long list of restrictions that impacted my personal freedom. Only as I got to know God did I discover that in fact I enjoyed the greatest of freedom. Sure there were boundaries, but I was invited to make my choices over the degree to which I maintained them. In the story of Adam and Eve we see the scale of God's generosity. His instruction was clear, 'You are free to eat from any tree in the garden; but you must not eat from the tree of the knowledge of good and evil, for when you eat from it you will certainly die.'[35] However, God entrusted the decision entirely to Adam.

God invites us to follow His instructions closely on the basis that they offer us our fullest personal fulfillment. The Bible, from start to finish, offers us clear guidance that will inevitably lead us into a deep and intimate friendship with God. Yet, along the way there are many distractions and a variety of perspectives which we will confront and need to deal with. Spiritual formation is learning how to take decisions that ensure we follow Jesus closely rather than become lost in a vast landscape of attractive and competing opportunities. For me this journey only became meaningful when I decided to take God at His word and live by his directions. This was in my mid-forties. It involved developing a discipline of resistance to where my natural appetites led me, appetites that present as persuasive arguments. Just as Satan persuaded Adam and Eve, whose decision led to the breach in their intimate relationship with God.[36]

SOMETHING TO CONSIDER: What appetites do you struggle with and which draw you away from God?

AN ACTION TO TAKE: Draw up a list of five key reasons why you want to grow to know God better. What prevents you from achieving these?

A PRAYER TO MAKE: 'Lord, I choose to walk in obedience to all that You have commanded. Help me to identify and resist the many distractions that draw me away from You.'

[35]Genesis 2:16b-17; [36]Genesis 3

Confidence in God

Being confident of this, that he who began a good work in you will carry it on to completion until the day of Christ Jesus.
Philippians 1:6

I've found it's all too easy to lose sight of God in life's many twists and turns. I remember going shopping with mum as a child. I'd get distracted by everything around me and lose sight of her. Then my heart beat faster, lost and alone amidst a sea of legs and arms.

Whilst I've no doubt God is working in my life, I experience real moments of self doubt over my spiritual growth. As the years have rolled on, my confidence has wavered. It's more difficult believing that my life shows practical signs of changing from one degree of glory to another.[37]

It may be that I'm disappointed and bewildered that after over forty years of following Jesus, I remain acutely aware of my human fracture. There are issues I have yet to master, issues I've consistently battled each one of those forty years.

My self-confidence has taken a hit, but that's no bad thing for my confidence in God continues to grow. The benefit is twofold; a fuller appreciation of God's forgiveness of my sin and His acceptance of me just as I am, and a far humbler attitude knowing I cannot change myself.

Consequently, I'm far more measured in my criticism of others. I think before I speak or act. It is one reason I have chosen the path of a contemplative committed to investing time and prayer in ordering my own life rather than seeking to fix the lives of others. It's been a difficult lesson learning that, whilst I can do nothing, God's Spirit can do immeasurably more than I can begin to imagine.[38] Making peace with my darker nature has meant owning and acknowledging it and accepting that all I can do is live with it within the grace God extends.

SOMETHING TO CONSIDER: Don't be discouraged if certain behaviours seem unbreakable.

AN ACTION TO TAKE: Acknowledge to God and yourself those fractures in your humanity that disappoint you and perhaps haunt you. Take time also to acknowledge that God loves you despite how you see yourself.

A PRAYER TO MAKE: 'Lord, please continue to bring to completion the good work seeded into my life and help me manage my misgivings and self-doubt well.'

[37]2 Corinthians 3:18 (See EDWJ Wed April 15th); [38]Ephesians 3:20-21

SUNDAY 18 APRIL

Christ is All

> **Therefore, since we are surrounded by such a great cloud of witnesses, let us throw off everything that hinders and the sin that so easily entangles. And let us run with perseverance the race marked out for us.** Hebrews 12:1

If ever life overwhelms me I stop to consider those Christians who have gone before me. It was the great Christian survivor of the Ravensbruck concentration camp, who said, 'Today I know that the experiences of our lives, when we let God use them, become the mysterious and perfect preparation for the work he will give us to do.'[39] When we find ourselves in a fix beyond our ability we can either panic, or entrust ourselves, fears and all, to God. I can invest my energy into telling God in prayer what needs to happen, or I can simply report for duty. This latter is what those who have established the long tradition of faithful followers of Jesus have done. When I cannot fathom my future, when all appears to be lost, it's time to reflect upon the lives of all those who have gone before me. None of them was perfect. King David, a man after God's own heart the Bible declares twice, was an adulterer and murderer. We are not to aim at perfection, but obedience.[40] This alone ensures we remain faithful to God, and we need not worry about the consequences. It's not that we shall avoid the worst of these, but we shall endure and emerge both wiser and better equipped to realise the God life within us. To quote Corrie again, 'You can never learn that Christ is all you need, until Christ is all you have.' Without doubt this is a scary place to be. Yet, in such situations we are to find our confidence in God's Word, 'In returning and rest you shall be saved; in quietness and in trust your strength lies.'[41] I've learnt to stop fretting and get on with completing the race that is mine to win.[42] The Christian life cannot guarantee calm seas and plain sailing, but does promise that I can discern God at each and every point of my life experience.

SOMETHING TO CONSIDER: How has God prepared you through life experience?

AN ACTION TO TAKE: Corrie Ten Boom forgave her enemies. Read this powerful story of forgiveness. Can you forgive those who may have hurt you in your life? Visit **edwj.org/ma21-18apr**[43]

A PRAYER TO MAKE: 'Lord, help me to find encouragement in the lives of those who have followed Jesus throughout history, and so find the strength to live through life's challenges.'

[39]Corrie Ten Boom, *The Hiding Place: The Triumphant True Story of Corrie Ten Boom*, (Hodder and Stoughton, 2012); [40]1 Samuel 13:14, Acts 13:22; [41]Isaiah 30:15; [42]1 Corinthians 9:23-27; [43]You can watch a film made of Corrie Ten Boom's life on YouTube; edwj.org/ma21-19apr

Christian Maturity

As a child, I talked like a child, I thought like a child, I reasoned like a child. When I became a man, I put childish ways behind me. For now we see only a reflection as in a mirror; then we shall see face to face. Now I know in part; then I shall know fully, even as I am fully known. 1 Corinthians 13:10-12

We have taken a week exploring Spiritual Formation, or how to grow up into maturity in Christ.[44] It is the goal of every follower of Jesus to become more like him and to pray the words of St. Richard of Chichester daily, 'My Lord Jesus Christ, may I know you more clearly, love you more dearly and follow you more nearly, day by day'. This process engages three distinct, yet interconnected, aspects of our life. The first is our thinking. Growing up we are surrounded by a multiplicity of ideas and we observe a variety of approaches to life. Consequently we form opinions about what's good and what's right. How can we judge which is best? For the disciple it is Scripture that offers us clear guidance and remains the source of Christian tradition and practice. Encountering Christ in the Bible will enable us to live as Jesus wants us to. The second is our emotions, for these will determine how we respond in life. Our feelings are strong drivers that rise within and easily overwhelm our capacity to think before we act. We are often left with regrets when we think through how we reacted and served our emotions rather than God's purpose in our life. Finally there is our behaviour, or putting our Christian understanding into practice. This clearly demonstrates that we are indeed living by God's Word in service in God's world. This is both at a personal and at a community level; loving God and loving neighbour. Life serves as a pilgrimage in which we journey towards God's heart through our diverse experiences. If we address our need to grow in God we shall engage as the Church in worship and service, establish a practical and meaningful devotional life and discover how to live out the God-life daily.

SOMETHING TO CONSIDER: Is what I say I believe reflected in my behaviour, feelings and relationships?

AN ACTION TO TAKE: Pick up a copy of *These Three Things* by Mick Brooks. Visit **waverleyabbeyresources.org/product/these-three-things**

A PRAYER TO MAKE: 'Lord, I desire to grow up into the fullest expression of Your love that I can. Help me to know You more clearly, love You more dearly and follow You more nearly every day.'

[44]Ephesians 4:14-16

TUESDAY 20 APRIL

Faith and Love

> **We always thank God, the Father of our Lord Jesus Christ, when we pray for you, because we have heard of your faith in Christ Jesus and of the love you have for all God's people.**
> Colossians 1:3-4

In reading the few surviving Christian texts from the second century, I'm struck by the importance of two small words: faith and love. St Ignatius of Antioch related them to the Eucharist and they were associated with the disciple's way of life.

I speak with people who know a lot about world religions, yet have questions about faith. All religions have belief systems and practices, yet these are insufficient to nurture or sustain faith. It presents the kernel that makes religion sustainable and purposeful. Without faith we can believe what we like, yet it exercises little influence on us apart from disciplined and repetitive practices. These may offer some comfort through familiarity, yet never the freedom and life that springs from faith in God.

Faith gives me confidence despite my questions. Whilst healthy, not all questions enjoy satisfactory answers. They deserve debate and scrutiny, yet in the knowledge that they may never be answered through rationality, or within our limited human capacity. In fact faith always retains a measure of mystery, for faith is born of trust, itself insubstantial. I give my trust with no guarantee that I won't be disappointed. Yet, I give it based upon an inner confidence that is only shaken when such trust is betrayed.

I've experienced many severe challenges and frustrations to my faith. I've also chosen to betray the trust God has placed in me. Yet, unlike me, God never chooses to withdraw the trust invested in me. I've lost count of the number of times I've returned to God, ashamed and sorry. This prodigal has disappeared to live amongst the pigs far too often.

SOMETHING TO CONSIDER: How does faith help you face the questions life presents you with?

AN ACTION TO TAKE: Read Hebrews 11 and write down what you learn about the way faith works in the life of a follower of Jesus.

A PRAYER TO MAKE: 'Lord, continue to nurture my faith that I might withstand the storms of life.'

Hope

The faith and love that spring from the hope stored up for you in heaven and about which you have already heard in the true message of the gospel that has come to you. Colossians 1:5-6A

Here in St Cuthbert's Oratory, a home of prayer, our three watchwords are hospitality, hope and healing – three gospel gifts we receive. God's hospitality welcomes us to our salvation banquet. What's more, He promised to feed us with bread for both stomach and spirit.

Hope sustains us through all eventualities. We do well to nurture it when things are stable for when storms sweep in, we have hope alone even as our lives are threatened. Healing is always the work of a lifetime as we seek to find our rest in God. I must learn to take the long view, when all I really want is a quick fix.

Incredibly, all three are always available to us for they've been wrestled from the devil's grasp by the cross.[45] We learn to draw upon the treasury of heaven, opened to us through Jesus' sacrificial death. It's why we pray, your Kingdom come, your will be done on earth, as it is in heaven.

It has taken me years to realise I'm not to plead for God's intervention. To do so is to miss the grace that is already mine in Christ. There are only three divine interventions; the crafting of order from chaos at the Creation, the redemption of humanity through Christ, and finally the return of Jesus at the end of time. So now I explore how to draw from heaven's treasure trove and discover how to live within its total provision for my daily necessities.

This is how I strengthen my understanding and exercise faith. This challenges how I've learnt to manage my expectations and experience. I must also nurture the love I have in my heart not simply for myself, but for everyone that Jesus came to serve.

SOMETHING TO CONSIDER: In what ways is your life offering hospitality, hope and healing to a world in need?

AN ACTION TO TAKE: Read *Love with Skin On*, in which Trevor Partridge explains how the Church, which is you and me, can come alongside people facing life's challenges. Visit **edwj.org/ma21-21apr**

A PRAYER TO MAKE: 'Lord, just as I receive hospitality, hope and healing from You may I offer it to those who I meet everyday.'

[45]Ephesians 4:7-13

THURSDAY 22 APRIL

Being Christian

So that you may live a life worthy of the Lord and please him in every way: bearing fruit in every good work, growing in the knowledge of God. Colossians 1:10

The earliest Christian writings emphasise human behaviour. Ignatius of Antioch writes, 'It is right, therefore, that we not just be called Christians, but that we actually be Christians'.[46] This is to live a life worthy of the Lord, our daily challenge.

I can reduce life to a set of performance targets, giving an impression of godliness but masking my struggles. Who wants their inner thoughts revealed to family and friends? Not that thoughts are sinful, yet they can prove harmful when entertained and allowed to give birth to aspirations and actions.

I live mostly inside my own head so I all too readily treat Christianity as a code of behaviour. If I keep it, I imagine myself holy. But this doesn't mean I'm happy. I find I must wrestle joyless internal feelings. Whilst maintaining the letter of the law I fail to grasp its spirit. Indeed, I considered ditching my faith three years in. Why? Well because it was such hard work. I was seeking to be a disciple and hadn't learnt that I needed to let go and let God.

I was helped by discovering that, like the Ephesian Christians, I'd been converted into the baptism of John for repentance so I hadn't heard of the Holy Spirit. In desperation, and exhausted in every aspect of my humanity, I surrendered to prayer and received the Holy Spirit. Things didn't get easier overnight. I remained the decision taker in all I thought and did. However, now I knew the presence of God in a fresh and compelling way.

The fruit from my life no longer needed to be manufactured through my own efforts. It was harvested from collaboration with the Spirit of God. I have come to realise that nothing compares to knowing Jesus. This is now my sole objective in the years I have left to me.

SOMETHING TO CONSIDER: What strategies have you developed to manage your struggle with temptation?

AN ACTION TO TAKE: Read Romans 7:14–8:39 and note how it connects with your life experience.

A PRAYER TO MAKE: 'Lord, thank You that there is absolutely nothing that can ever separate me from Your love.'

[46] Letter to the Magnesisans, 4

Perseverance

Being strengthened with all power according to his glorious might so that you may have great endurance and patience, and giving joyful thanks to the Father, who has qualified you to share in the inheritance of his holy people in the kingdom of light.
Colossians 1:11-12

Life is a marathon not a sprint. I've a friend who, as a child, wondered why adults always walked. In contrast she joyfully ran everywhere and promised herself she'd continue running once an adult. Sadly the ageing process had its way, and childhood pledges made way for adult realities.

I've never been a sprinter. I was always a middle distance runner. Rather than explosive speed, I build up and endure the greater distance. I believe that to navigate the Christian life we must be long distance runners. The challenge is completing the race, and here pace counts for everything.

Before ever running in competition I remember pounding the school track with my trainer timing me, checking my pulse rate at the start and conclusion of each circuit, teaching me to manage my energy better. He also taught me never to envisage the finish until I hit the final bend. It was also important I ran my race and no-one elses.

In the Christian life, each of us needs a race plan and the perseverance to complete the course. Good news! All such resources are made freely available in Jesus. Yet, so much will depend on my mood and mindset. I must take responsibility and manage myself effectively. I can't just expect to do well. Running also taught me that sacrifice was required if I was to compete effectively.

With the Holy Spirit as our trainer we will discover how to run our life's race well. There will be times when injury precludes us from full participation. Yet, when we treat injuries appropriately we recover, ready to participate once again.

SOMETHING TO CONSIDER: Are you ready to get fit for the race of your life?

AN ACTION TO TAKE: Consult a book to grow in relationship with God and race for Jesus. Visit **edwj.org/ma21-23apr**

A PRAYER TO MAKE: 'Lord, strengthen me so I might persevere through my life's race.'

SATURDAY 24 APRIL
Non-Performance

For he has rescued us from the dominion of darkness and brought us into the kingdom of the Son he loves, in whom we have redemption, the forgiveness of sins. Colossians 1:13–14

C hristianity is not a performance industry. God has no interest in our performance, which is something we manufacture for some purpose we perceive is beneficial to us. Performance measures how well I do something. This is not the measure God applies. Our friendship with God is only possible because of what Jesus has won for us on Calvary. No matter what I do I can add nothing to the grace gift extended to me by God. Often I have attempted to win God's approval. Or worse, I have compared myself favourably against what I determine is another person's failure. Christianity is not graded like an exam, from outstanding to failure.

That's because we all start out as failures. We don't have the ability to put things right with God. That's the work of redemption and we are the beneficiaries of a love that knows no bounds. It's our choice the degree to which we place our faith in God no matter what hand life deals us. For through the eye of faith we see God's purpose and realise our destiny.

Without faith we can only rely upon our performance, assuming it impresses God as much as we might impress ourselves. Those with no faith often appeal to their attempt to live a good life as their deposit against an eternity they're not sure they believe in. Sadly, the best of lives make no impression upon a God who sent his own Son to recover us from the dominion of darkness.

Faith is non-transferable. It is the prize awaiting anyone who has the courage to embark upon a quest in search of a faith of their own. As with every quest, such adventures are fraught with dangers, difficulties and doubts. What might best be described as the shadow of faith.

SOMETHING TO CONSIDER: How effectively has the seed of faith planted in your heart grown over your years of following Jesus? Is it in need of some attention?

AN ACTION TO TAKE: Acknowledge that there is nothing you can do that will make you worthier of God's love.

A PRAYER TO MAKE: 'Lord, thank You for rescuing me from the dominion of darkness and forgiving me my sins.'

Once you were alienated from God and were enemies in your minds because of your evil behaviour. But now he has reconciled you by Christ's physical body through death to present you holy in his sight, without blemish and free from accusation. Colossians 1:21–22

One of my most challenging experiences was to visit refugee camps. I met people who had nothing, completely dependent on the goodwill of others. Their human spirit revealed itself in the ways they managed their daily lives. Yet some grew despondent, seeing daily life as a fruitless distraction from their responsibility in securing their family's future safety.

My life is unremarkable by comparison. I've enjoyed a stable background, academic success and freedom of expression. I've encountered unwelcome events, but overall I've managed life OK. I've not needed rescuing apart from our shared human need to escape the consequences of sin and separation from God. Even this was a pretty simple journey. I embraced Christianity, made my home in the church and enjoyed the benefits of fellowship and faith. I never experienced the acute sense of anxiety of those I met in refugee camps. So I took my Christian faith for granted with its privileged citizenship in God's Kingdom. No longer stateless, I had a purpose and a future.

During the long weeks of lockdown I had opportunity to consider just how grateful I am for the love of God that saved a wretch like me. I have always gladly responded to God's love, yet struggled with faith until I faced the reality of my sin. Comparison with others, so often my source of self justification, was irrelevant, for I had no less need of grace than the greatest sinner on earth. I've slowly come to value the scale of God's rescue and surrendered completely to God's love.

SOMETHING TO CONSIDER: Where have you encountered God's love in your life this week?

AN ACTION TO TAKE: Is there some step that requires an act of faith in your life? What stops you from taking that step?

A PRAYER TO MAKE: 'Lord, present me holy in Your sight, without blemish and free from accusation.'

MONDAY 26 APRIL

Faith and Fear

If you continue in your faith, established and firm, and do not move from the hope held out in the gospel. This is the gospel that you heard and that has been proclaimed to every creature under heaven, and of which I, Paul, have become a servant.

Colossians 1:23

C hristrianity is about learning to stay true to one's decision to follow Jesus. Life has its ways of testing our resolve. There is good precedent since all the disciples abandoned Jesus at His arrest. This abandonment wasn't a reflection of their love, rather an acknowledgment of their fear and uncertainty. Faith will always have a shadow of fear to accompany it. For faith cannot be established beyond reasonable doubt. Indeed, it is the very fact of doubt that nurtures faith. We have to decide if we can, and will, trust God despite circumstances that apparently deny the truth we lay claim to.

Fortunately we only have to find faith for the immediate circumstances of our own life. So it is idle speculation to fear martyrdom when martyrdom is currently rare, even unheard of, across the UK. Yet, we can never experience love without faith. Even at a human level love demands I take a risk with my emotions and my commitment. There always remains the chance that such love will fail leaving me with some hard questions to work through. Married to someone who has been through a divorce, the injury to faith in a promise is deep and long lasting once broken. This is because faith can never be guaranteed. Activating it requires risk, and risk always exposes us to danger. Christianity is a dangerous path to follow. It will test our resilience at every level of our being. It is said that the older we get the more risk averse we become. The great danger here is that we fail to run with perseverance the race of faith. The temptation to settle, an invitation that society appears to present with the illusion of a comfortable retirement, is a deceit that if followed may rob following generations of witnessing how we live by faith up to and beyond the threshold of death.

SOMETHING TO CONSIDER: How risk averse are you by nature?

AN ACTION TO TAKE: Read Genesis 12–13 and discover how faith fuels an effective retirement. Abraham was 75 years old!

A PRAYER TO MAKE: 'Lord, let me never lose sight or let go of the hope born of faith throughout my life.'

God With Us

All your works praise you, Lord; your faithful people extol you.
Psalm 145:10

In our home, I love our garden. The autumn presents a stunning display, a plethora of colours. The bare boughs of winter, stark against the bleak skies, contrasts with the bud and fresh flowers of springtime. Always alive, it declares God's unsearchable character. We run a retreat called 'Eyes Wide Open'. It offers an opportunity to find God's presence in the sights and sounds of nature. As St. Paul reminds us, '... all creation has been groaning as in the pains of childbirth right up to the present time.'[47] We explore God's presence that consistently surrounds us.

My approach to life changed when I opened my eyes to God's reality in everything; in the waxing and waning of the seasons, alive in the natural expressions of the landscape that enfolds me. Here, whatever my mood, I pause, break state and encounter God in the immediacy of my surroundings. For too long my attention was consumed with events. I lost sight of God and lived two lives; one in which I prayed and read Scripture, the other working through my daily agenda. It took sometime to adjust to the fact that God is always present, and when I was lost, God's creation can reveal God's reality. No wonder creation groans with our lack of attentiveness to God's ever present majesty.

In both the vastness of space, with the night sky populated with thousands of stars, or quietly gazing upon a flower, I'm reminded of the unfathomable riches that are mine in Jesus. Life seeks to squeeze God's life out of me. If I overthink my faith I get lost in rational arguments both for and against God. Yet, when I'm attentive to the expression of God in all that surrounds me, I join with God's works in giving thanks for the simple fact of God. Creation with its seasonal procession of colours is a silent provocation to each one of us to praise God, whatever season of life we find ourselves experiencing.

SOMETHING TO CONSIDER: Do you need to open your eyes wide and learn to worship God afresh?

AN ACTION TO TAKE: A retreat offers a great way to place life on pause and encounter God. Visit **edwj.org/ma21-27apr**

A PRAYER TO MAKE: 'Lord, I lift up my voice and praise You with all Your works.'

[47]Romans 8:22-24

WEDNESDAY 28 APRIL

Eternity

Your kingdom is an everlasting kingdom, and your dominion endures through all generations. Psalm 145:13

Considering eternity, I'm challenged by the quote, 'Many long for eternity, when they don't know what to do on a wet Sunday afternoon'.[48] I can quickly grow bored but pursuing a prayerful life has, with twists and turns, brought me into a space where I can't remember experiencing boredom. I'm no saint, but time is now my friend and not something I struggle with. Is this age-related? As I interact with my peers I hear stories of 'being at a loose end'. The great thing about God's forever Kingdom is that it expresses its partial shape here on earth. It's not awaiting Jesus' second coming but begins the moment we yield to Jesus. Now we navigate mortality with the Kingdom both present and ahead of us. I've learnt I can live my life three ways. The first only requires me to serve the letter of the Christian Law. Church attendance and affirming biblical truths, whilst I simply live as I choose. There is always a shadow of deceit, of self and others, as I refuse to live an authentic faith born of my personal battles. A second, and more honest, approach is to let life happen and spend my time reacting to my circumstances. This is exhausting and only ever reveals the worst aspects of my character. This is because I am reacting from my own sentiments created by my situation. These may feel like my true feelings, but are in fact no more than my preferences in reaction to what I don't like.

Finally, I can acknowledge my immediate reaction without choosing to express it. Here I might pause and review the landscape I'm entering into and take a moment to discover Jesus now; Jesus as Jesus is and not as I might like Jesus to be. I resist running away in fear and anger nor grudgingly accepting my lot as some sacrificial victim.

SOMETHING TO CONSIDER: How do you choose to live your life in God?

AN ACTION TO TAKE: Help build God's Kingdom by the choices you make. You're invited to gaze upon God, and as this becomes your practice so all other distractions and diversions become nothing other than unwelcome interruptions.

A PRAYER TO MAKE: 'Lord, may Your Kingdom come and Your will be done on earth in and through my life.'

[48]Susan Ertz, 1887-198

The Lord upholds all who fall and lifts up all who are bowed down. The eyes of all look to you, and you give them their food at the proper time. Psalm 145:14–15

I don't know if you have ever tried lifting someone who doesn't enjoy control over their muscles and limbs? I have when working as a carer. Because they could not cooperate with my attempts to lift them, I was lifting a 'dead weight'. It was an impossible task. The psalmist reminds me that I have to cooperate with God rather than assume that God will deliver me from discomforting situations.

We enjoy a real relationship with God, and whilst occasionally I am incapable of cooperating, most times it's a case of finding the determination and resilience to press on. Having walked with God for over forty years, only recently have I begun to resist my inner angst from deciding my reaction, mood and spiritual condition. Faced with the unpalatable, I catastrophize my situation and choose panic over faith. Choosing faith offers no obvious road out of my challenge, yet it always directs my gaze back to God, my rescuer.

In my experience it's 'in the squeeze', when my fears rise and I struggle to maintain a positive outlook, that spiritual growth takes place. It's my declared ambition to grow up into maturity in Christ, yet I never calculated the reality of how that squeeze would reveal the poverty of my spiritual capacity. I found I had little more than a series of confident statements that were blown apart in the face of the slightest obstruction. I had to learn to live within the substance of God's promise, for here alone is the source of that promise, God, to be found. It's one reason why reading Scripture is so essential for it is indeed the only food that nourishes faith and carries us into intimate friendship with God. We discover how to live where others fear to tread.

SOMETHING TO CONSIDER: How difficult is it for you to find God in every situation?

AN ACTION TO TAKE: Read the *Cover to Cover* booklet on the Lord's Prayer and learn how to grow in your spiritual life. Visit **edwj.org/ma21-29apr**

A PRAYER TO MAKE: 'Lord, support me when I stumble and lift me up when I fall.'

FRIDAY 30 APRIL

Discernment

You open your hand and satisfy the desires of every living thing. The Lord is righteous in all his ways and faithful in all he does.

Psalm 145:16–17

Discernment is essential in following Jesus. It's distinguishing between reality and personal preference. Often, what I discern is not as appetising as what I'd like. So for me, following Jesus did not include experiencing personal emotional and psychological pain. Yet, on reflection this yielded a richer experience of God's presence and reality.

I'm not equating pain with spiritual growth. Yet, there are life events that, depending on how we address them, will either draw us closer to God or drive us from God. In fact my discernment process does both initially; my longing for more of God remains real even as I'm confronted by pain. Here I argue with God and may turn my back on him.

When young, my dad would hold out two clenched hands to me, inviting me to choose. One contained a sweet, the other was empty. Yet, sometimes he held a gift in both. I chose, and couldn't guarantee what I'd get. However, having guessed wrong, dad still let me have a second bite of the cherry, and I secured my reward. So it is with God. In turning my back I cannot see two extended arms each with a clenched hand concealing a surprise. However, once I've worked through my indignation, rage and fear and turn back to God, I have the opportunity to discover God's way, even though my initial decision and course of action may offer little immediate reward.

I only discover my freedom in the provision that comes from God's hand. Circumstances don't change; my attitude and perspective do. What I initially experience as God's unkindness is really a means to deepening my understanding of God and myself. So discerning, that is distinguishing the blessing in the pain, is a critical exercise we are all invited to experience.

SOMETHING TO CONSIDER: Does God appear unfair to you? If so, do you feel wounded?

AN ACTION TO TAKE: Revisit a painful episode and write down how and what it made you feel. Over time were there new opportunities that emerged?

A PRAYER TO MAKE: 'Lord, at times I find You to be unfair. Help me to discern what You have in Your hand for my nourishment in such seasons.'

Order form

Get Your **FREE** Daily Bible Reading Notes **TODAY!** (UK ONLY)

Your favourite Bible Reading notes are now available to you for FREE. God has called us back to the original vision of CWR to provide these notes to everyone who needs them, regardless of their circumstance or ability to pay. It is our desire to see these daily bible reading notes used more widely, to see Christians grow in their relationship with Jesus on a daily basis and to see Him reflected in their everyday living. More than 60,000 copies each year are delivered into prisons too and our vision is to grow this ministry even further, putting these notes into the hands of those in challenging situations and to see their lives transformed through a new and growing relationship with Jesus. Clearly there are costs to provide this ministry and we are trusting in God's provision.

Could you be part of this vision? Do you have the desire to see lives transformed through a relationship with Jesus? **A small donation from you of just £2 a month, by direct debit, will make such a difference** Giving hope to someone in desperate need whilst you too grow deeper in your own relationship with Jesus.

4 Easy Ways To Order

1. Visit our online store at **waverleyabbeyresources.org/store**
2. Send this form together with your payment to:
   CWR, Waverley Abbey House, Waverley Lane, Farnham, Surrey GU9 8EP
3. Phone in your credit card order: **01252 784700** (Mon–Fri, 9.30am – 4.30pm)
4. Visit a Christian bookshop

For a list of our National Distributors, who supply countries outside the UK, visit waverleyabbeyresources.org/distributors

Your Details (required for orders and donations)

Full Name: _____ CWR ID No. (if known): _____

Home Address: _____

Postcode: _____

Telephone No. (for queries): _____ Email: _____

Publications

TITLE	QTY	PRICE	TOTAL
	Total Publications		

UK P&P: up to £24.99 = **£2.99**; £25.00 and over = **FREE**	
Elsewhere P&P: up to £10 = **£4.95**; £10.01 – £50 = **£6.95**; £50.01 – £99.99 = **£10**; £100 and over = **£30**	
Total Publications and P&P (please allow 14 days for delivery) **A**	

Payment Details

☐ I enclose a cheque made payable to CWR for the amount of: **£** _____

☐ Please charge my credit/debit card.

Cardholder's Name (in BLOCK CAPITALS) _____

Card No. ☐☐☐☐ ☐☐☐☐ ☐☐☐☐ ☐☐☐☐

Expires End ☐☐ ☐☐   Security Code ☐☐☐

Continued overleaf >>

One off Special Gift to CWR ☐ Please send me an acknowledgement of my gift **B**

GRAND TOTAL (Total of A & B)

Gift Aid (your home address required, see overleaf)

giftaid it I am a UK taxpayer and want CWR to reclaim the tax on all my donations for the four years prior to this year **and on** all donations I make from the date of this Gift Aid declaration until further notice.*

Taxpayer's Full Name (in BLOCK CAPITALS) _____

Signature _____ **Date** _____

*I am a UK taxpayer and understand that if I pay less Income Tax and/or Capital Gains Tax than the amount of Gift Aid claimed on all my donations in that tax year it is my responsibility to pay any difference.

Your FREE Daily Bible Reading Notes Order

	Please Tick FREE	£2 pcm	£5 pcm	£10 pcm	Other
Every Day with Jesus (1yr, 6 issues)	☐	☐	☐	☐	☐ £ _____
Large Print *Every Day with Jesus* (1yr, 6 issues)	☐	☐	☐	☐	☐ £ _____
Inspiring Women Every Day (1yr, 6 issues)	☐	☐	☐	☐	☐ £ _____

All CWR Bible reading notes are also available in single issue **ebook** and **email subscription** format. Visit **waverleyabbeyresources.org** for further info.

CWR Instruction to your Bank or Building Society to pay by Direct Debit

DIRECT Debit

Please fill in the form and send to: CWR, Waverley Abbey House, Waverley Lane, Farnham, Surrey GU9 8EP

Name and full postal address of your Bank or Building Society

To: The Manager _____ Bank/Building Society

Address _____

_____

_____

Postcode _____

Name(s) of Account Holder(s)

Branch Sort Code

Bank/Building Society Account Number

Originator's Identification Number

4	2	0	4	8	7

Reference

Instruction to your Bank or Building Society

Please pay CWR Direct Debits from the account detailed in this Instruction subject to the safeguards assured by the Direct Debit Guarantee. I understand that this Instruction may remain with CWR and, if so, details will be passed electronically to my Bank/Building Society.

Signature(s)

_____

_____

Date

Banks and Building Societies may not accept Direct Debit Instructions for some types of account

For a subscription outside of the UK please visit www.waverleyabbeyresources.org where you will find a list of our national distributors.

How would you like to hear from us? We would love to keep you up to date on all aspects of the CWR ministry, including; new publications, events & courses as well as how you can support us.

If you **DO** want to hear from us on email, please tick here [ ]   If you **DO NOT** want us to contact you by post, please tick here [ ]

You can update your preferences at any time by contacting our customer services team on 01252 784 700.   You can view our privacy policy online at waverleyabbeyresources.org